CODE NAME: KING KONG

It was a fitting name for the giant Dutch Resistance leader. King Kong had the most dangerous job of all—that of a double agent. A few months before the Allied landing at Arnhem, he had finally managed to infiltrate Nazi counterintelligence.

After the bloody combat of "Operation Market Garden"—the Arnhem invasion—King Kong was accused of selling out. Was he the traitor who changed the ending of World War II?

For the first time in thirty years this book reopens the files, piecing together the truth behind the invasion at Arnhem with a vividness you will never forget! Here is the full, true story behind this epic battle—a bloody conflict marked by intrigue, double-dealing and betrayal!

BETRAYAL AT ARNHEM

A. Laurens

Translated from the French by
Sarah C. Crouch

CHARTER
NEW YORK

AWARD BOOKS ARE PUBLISHED BY
UNIVERSAL-AWARD HOUSE, INC.
DISTRIBUTED BY ACE BOOKS
A DIVISION OF CHARTER COMMUNICATIONS INC.
A GROSSET & DUNLAP COMPANY

Charter Books
A Division of Charter Communications Inc.
A Grosset & Dunlap Company
360 Park Avenue South
New York, New York 10010

i

2 4 6 8 0 9 7 5 3 1
Manufactured in the United States of America

A Strategic Position

In the Autumn of 1944, the Allied armies, racing across Europe in an all-out effort to end the war by Christmas, faced a stalemate. A bridgehead was needed for a concentrated assault on one sector of the front; an airborne strike into German-held Holland might turn the tide by forcing a gap in the defenses of the Nazis.

Ten thousand men were dropped around the city of Arnhem—a city on the Rhine near the German border (see map following)—by glider and parachute. Over *seven thousand* were killed or taken prisoner by the Germans. Someone had talked and Arnhem became a synonym for betrayal . . .

THE NETHERLANDS

BETRAYAL AT ARNHEM

CHAPTER ONE

Major Friedrich Kiesewetter, commanding officer of Abwehr IIIF (counterespionage German Military Intelligence), put down his fork and looked over at his luncheon guest.

"Well," he demanded a bit impatiently, "what do you think?"

But *Kriminalrat Sturmbannfuhrer* SS Joseph Schreieder, Gestapo Chief at the Hague, was in no rush to answer. He was enjoying his lunch—and his "dear friend" Kiesewetter's discomfort—and thinking enviously that the major had been lucky in his choice of headquarters in Holland. Dreibergen—near Utrecht, Arnhem and the Zuiderzee—was a picturesque tourist village set in a wooded, hilly region not far from the Dutch-German border.

It was almost noon, Sunday September 17, 1944. Nearby, an anti-aircraft battery suddenly opened fire, but neither officer paid any attention to the noise. Allied aircraft had been busy all night and all morning, flying over Holland to attack their targets in Germany. For that day's air operations, the British Meteorological Office had correctly predicted fine weather after the early morning mists dispersed.

"I think, my dear Keisewetter," Schreieder said, finally

answering the major, "that there can no longer be any doubt about it. The Allies are planning a major offensive in this area!"

Kiesewetter sighed. It certainly looked like it, and that was the problem: there were too many clues pointing that way.

(1) The Allied ground forces' build-up along the Belgian-Dutch border had been the subject of dozens of reports that had reached Kiesewetter's desk.

(2) The Luftwaffe had picked up transmissions from RAF and USAAF planes and had reported that these forces were preparing for action.

(3) Finally, just two days before, two RAF aircraft screened by a protective escort of 30 Marauder fighters had flown over the Arnhem-Nijmegen area— as if the Allied military leaders were personally surveying the future battleground.

It was all too open, too easy, and it bothered an old intelligence hand like Kiesewetter. Could it be a trick? Could it be what the Allies wanted them to believe and concentrate on while they prepared to attack somewhere else . . . perhaps even inside Germany?

Gestapo Chief Schreieder was prepared to accept the obvious. "No doubt about it," he repeated. "Arnhem . . . Eindhoven, that is the target. This latest information you have received confirms it."

And that *really* worried Kiesewetter. In the final analysis, everything seemed to depend on the word of one man. A "turncoat," Christiaan Lindemans, known to the Dutch Resistance as "King Kong" and "Krist" and to the Abwehr, which had recently recruited him, as "C.C."

Two days before, Lindemans had shown up at Dreibergen with a copy of a message from the British forces to the members of the Dutch Resistance, altering them to wait for weapons and instructions which would shortly be dispatched to them. The Resistance was also asked to keep all downed Allied pilots and escaped prisoners it was presently hiding in Holland, instead of guiding them to the Allied lines as they had been doing.

This seemed to imply that a general offensive was about to be launched. It also seemed to confirm information received on the twenty-fifth of August by the Belgian White Army that Field Marshal Bernard Montgomery planned to attack Dina, Nijmegen and Arnhem inside Holland, as well as strike along the Issel River and the German coast of the North Sea.

"Well, Keisewetter?" Now it was Schreieder's turn to be impatient.

The major shrugged. "Perhaps Lindemans is telling the truth. Certainly Willy Bittrich [Lt. Gen. Wilhelm Bittrich] thinks the target is Arnhem. On the other hand, perhaps we are deliberately being misled and the paratroopers will land somewhere else . . . in Germany say, the way Model [Field Marshal Walter Model] thinks?"

"Surely that is rather too subtle," said Schreieder, showing the Gestapo's usual disdain of its rival service.

"Subtle?" Kiesewetter smiled. "Not for Montgomery. I believe that he is capable of almost anything. Remember the trick he played on us when he pretended to be aiming for Sardinia and then landed—unmolested—in Sicily? Remember how he mounted a gigantic camouflage, pretending to be disembarking in the Pas-de-Calais, when he and Eisenhower were already commanding the invasion of Normandy?"

The major paused, shaking his head. "No, Montgomery is capable of anything. A plan to trick us into believing that he will attack Arnhem, when he really intends to drop his troops inside Germany, would be very much in character. I can't afford to make a mistake. A diversionary attack could very easily trick us into bringing our whole army into Holland, leaving the way to Berlin exposed and defenseless."

"What does Giskes think?" Schreieder asked, referring to the major's CO, Lt. Col. Hermann Giskes.

"*Colonel* Giskes," said Kiesewetter coldly, "is as pleased as punch. 'C.C.' is one of his favorites. After all, he personally recruited him."

If he hadn't been speaking to an officer in the Gestapo, Kiesewetter might have added that he thought Colonel Giskes was *too* fond of C.C. to be relied on to give an unbiased opinion of the agent's reliability. Giskes considered himself a "natural" in counterespionage—and he had had some notable successes. He had begun his career as a company officer during WWI, worked his way up through the Abwehr to his present high position under Adolf Hitler and was a very good friend of Field Marshal Gerd von Rundstedt.

But, was Giskes right this time? Was Lindemans worthy of his trust? Did the young Dutchman really serve the Abwehr as devotedly as his mentor believed or had he infiltrated on orders of the Resistance to spread confusion? What was he—traitor or patriot? "Turned" agent or double agent?

Schreieder had met Lindemans and Kiesewetter had wanted the Gestapo chief's opinion of him, but now he was sorry he had invited the man to lunch. He did not like Schreieder, and he had plenty of company. A small, fat man with a bald head that seemed to rest on the collar of his uniform and small, protruding eyes in a large pale face that made him look like the rat he was reputed to be, Schreieder was not liked by anyone.

Now his chubby, well-manicured hands waved aside Kiesewetter's questions. "I was not with Lindemans long enough to form an accurate impression of him," he protested. "He struck me as an impulsive young man, rather vague, brutal, but that is all I can tell you."

That was that. They continued the meal in silence, a silence unbroken until an aide hurried in and whispered to Kiesewetter that Allied paratroopers had landed near Eindhoven, resolving the major's dilemma dramatically.

That Sunday morning at his headquarters in Vught, near Eindhoven, set up in a charming country house belonging to a man named Neuningen, General Kurt Student had been thinking about Christiaan Lindemans, too. There had been nothing in the agent's report to convince him that the Allies weren't laying the groundwork for another trick. He had confirmed in his report to Field Marshal Model that an attack on Holland looked imminent, but it would not be an airborne operation.

That day had dawned quiet in Student's area, but activity in the air gradually increased. By midday, the racket had become so intense that Student put down the files he was studying and went out to see what was happening.

Standing on his balcony he saw—very high up at first—a cloud of fighters and bombers. Then came the enormous transports, some flying in formation, others arriving singly—a continuous wave of aircraft.

Student, commander of Germany's First Parachute Army
—the footsoldiers of the Luftwaffe—and the remnants of the
15th Army (60,000 men who had just barely escaped capture by the Allies at Antwerp) watched, fascinated.

Turning to an officer who joined him on the balcony, he
commented admiringly on the size of the airborne operation,
forgetting in his excitement that it was *his* forces who were
under attack.

Field Marshal Walter Model had been based at Oosterbeek,
at the Tafelberg Hotel, since September 15. His headquarters
was only two kilometers from Arnhem on the Utrecht road.

Hitler had nicknamed Model "the victor of the East front."
Now the Field Marshal was preparing to attack the West
front. A merciless, impatient, decisive man of fifty, Model
owed his position as much to his success in battle as to his
friendship with the Führer. He was considered to be a brutal
but practical tactician, more in favor of defensive action than
offensive.

Well aware of the movement of Allied troops along the
Belgian-Dutch border, frustrated by contradictory information received from his various sources, Model acted out possible Allied attack plans in his imagination. He concluded
that the 2nd British Division would attack his right wing in
the Ruhr, near Roxermond. The left wing, he guessed, would
cross the Waal River at Nijmegen, at the same time encircling
the German forces in the Dutch coastal areas. Now certain
that the information he had been getting had at least some
truth to it, Model decided to turn his own paratroopers south,
towards Münster.

Yet, only a few days before, when General Hans Rauter,
Polizei Führer of Holland, asked him if an Allied airborne
attack was very likely, Model had laughed at the idea. He
thought he knew Montgomery well enough to be quite certain
that he would not send his precious troops into an offensive
which—until the port of Antwerp was secured—would be
extremely dangerous. His opinion was that Montgomery "on
the tactical level is a very prudent man." The objective was
surely too far away from present Allied supply bases to have
any chance of success.

"And that is why, my dear Rauter," Model concluded, his chief of staff, Lt. Gen. Hans Krebs nodding agreement, "we are convinced that our headquarters at Oosterbeek will remain safe and sound."

At about one o'clock on Sunday afternoon, September 17, Model was forced to change his tune. Nearby, Allied paratroopers were falling from the sky like rain. When Model was informed, he gave the order to transfer his command post to General Bittrich's area.

As Model was giving this order, Krebs was called to the phone. At their headquarters in Hilversum, a gracious old watering town which had been rudely shaken out of its usual peacefulness, Von Wulich (head of the German Military Administration in occupied Holland since 1940) and Luftwaffe general Friedrich Christiansen had just been informed of the attack on Arnhem. They wanted to know if the report was true.

"Oh, yes, it's true all right," Krebs told them, adding: "We're right in the middle of the drop. If we don't change our position immediately, we'll all be taken prisoner!"

After the first shock wore off, General Christiansen, who had fulfilled his career properly but without particular glory, decided to relax and let Model do the worrying about the attack.

"After all," he thought, "it's really more his business than mine . . ."

At Oosterbeek, where the Park Hotel and the Tafelberg Hotel were being evacuated by the Germans, there was total confusion. Model and his staff ran to their rooms and threw a few things into their bags—leaving many top secret files behind in their haste to escape.

A car was waiting for Model. As he ran toward it, his case fell open, the contents spilling on the ground. Clumsy hands went to the Field Marshal's assistance. Panic was beginning to set in.

At last the convoy was formed. It would stop first at Arnhem to drop off a replacement for the commanding officer who had been killed in the attack. Its final destination was Doetincham and General de Waffen SS Wilhelm "Willy" Bittrich's command post.

Bittrich, a handsome young man reputed to be both intelligent and courageous, had been the only high-ranking officer in Holland who believed there would be an Allied airborne attack.

At the beginning of September, there had been only a few scattered units of German troops in Holland. On September 8, these were joined by four divisions equipped with tanks and mobile guns—some of these mounted on the undercarriages of Panther tanks. These forces included the 9th and 10th Divisions of the II SS Panzer Corps. Until diverted to Arnhem, one of these had been scheduled to return to Germany from France; the other was preparing to leave Denmark. On the day of the Arnhem drop, Bittrich was put in command of all these forces—with the backing of Berlin and over the opposition of Model and Student.

What had alerted Bittrich—long before Christiaan Lindemans arrived at Abwehr headquarters in Dreibergen—to Allied plans when they must still have been in their infancy? How was he able to form a formidable armored force in Holland without the intelligence service of SHAEF—Supreme Headquarters Allied Expeditionary Forces—being alerted?

Of all the reasons for the debacle at Arnhem, the most important was the loss of the element of surprise. Somebody had betrayed the Allies' plans to the Germans. But the betrayer could not have been Christiaan Lindemans. By the time he had entered the picture, everything had been already set in motion.

Was it possible that he had been used as a scapegoat? Had Christiaan Lindemans betrayed his country, or was he an innocent victim, sacrificed to cover up for the real traitor?

CHAPTER TWO

If the airborne attack on Arnhem had succeeded, it is almost certain that the Germans would have been defeated before the end of the winter of 1944, thereby saving many thousands of lives and shortening the war by almost a year.

During the summer of 1944, the Germans were on the run, retreating across France. By the end of August, the Allies realized their pursuing armies could not keep up the pace, despite the disorganization of the *Wehrmacht* fleeing before them. Supplies were not reaching them fast enough or in large enough quantities from the Normandy beachheads. It seemed a choice had to be made: wait for the supplies to be replenished and then launch an all-out offensive all along the front, or concentrate their strength on a narrow front in what Gen. Dwight D. Eisenhower, commanding the Allied forces, called an "offensive as pointed as a pencil."

Eisenhower himself had always favored a broad front strategy. But that front now extended from the English Channel to Switzerland. Soon it would extend as far as Marseille. It was obvious that, given the current supply situation, the Allies could not keep up the same pressure on the Germans all along the line.

Field Marshal Bernard Montgomery, at a meeting with Eisenhower on August 23, pushed for an all-out attack *now* on a narrow front.

"We must," Monty argued, "stop the advance on the right and strike with the left, or stop the advance on the left and strike with the right. We must choose the place for an offensive and lean on it with all our strength. For, if we scatter our material resources and advance on a wide front, we will be so weak everywhere that we won't have the slightest chance of success."

Monty wanted to take his British and Canadian forces, plus all the men and supplies Ike could give him, on a concentrated drive through Belgium and Holland, around the northern tip of the German "Siegfried Line" into the Ruhr—Germany's industrial heartland—and, if all went well, on to Berlin.

The plan, Eisenhower felt, was too ambitious. Temporizer and diplomat, he opted for a compromise, what amounted to a broad front strategy but with limited objectives. His northern wing had to capture a good supply port before throwing itself across the Rhine and into the strategic Ruhr, which furnished 51.7 percent of the carbon and 50.4 percent of the steel for the Third Reich's war machine.

At the same time, in the south, General George S. Patton, commanding the American Third Army, after joining forces with the Sixth Franco-American Army coming up from the Mediterranean coast, would keep the pressure on the Germans in the vital Saar region.

While refusing to go along with Monty's battle plan, Ike did agree to give him certain priorites in men and supplies to capture the port the Allies need so badly. He would have the use of the Allied First Airborne Division, based in England; the support of the U.S. First Army on his right and first call on certain supplies.

Montgomery was disappointed, but Eisenhower would not bend. Added to the military reasons for his decision were political motives which, by the way, he did not try to hide. If he stopped Patton to give the main chance to Monty, "public opinion (American) would not put up with it" and "it is the public which wins wars."

Ike made the point that Patton was still popular with the American public (which was not at all certain) and that Montgomery was not (which was indisputable). Ralph Ingersoll, an American war correspondent on the Western Front, expressed perfectly the average American's sentiment when he said: "Montgomery is a general whom we do not like. We find him arrogant, presumptuous, antipathetic, and badly brought up."

In fact, Monty was the antithesis of what a general should be to win American hearts. His men, however, loved him— because he was direct, because he could explain a complicated problem simply and because he had a sense of humor.

On the eve of the Normandy landings, for example, to raise the morale of his troops he declared: "I know that you will follow me with joy." When the response was rather less than enthusiastic, he added quickly: "Ah! But you don't know where I want to go—I want to go home!" Which earned him the cheer "dear old Monty!" over and over again.

Unfortunately, Montgomery, thanks to his blunt nature, was not popular with his equals or superiors.

Added to this personality conflict was a fundamental difference in strategic conception among the Allied commanders. The Americans believed in the superiority of numbers—of men and material: "steam roller" tactics, in short, although their Allies never put it quite that way.

Bernard Montgomery had an infinitely more subtle mind. He enjoyed, in common with Winston Churchill, making unexpected use of new inventions. He believed in speed, surprise, intelligence and the final triumph of the mind over crude material.

But Monty had his orders and on August 29, 1944, he received permission to start the northern advance again, to gain on the retreating Germans who, once across the Somme River, might recover if they were given time.

The XXX Corps, commanded by Lt. General Brian Horrocks, a tall thin man with white hair, a penetrating look and the unexpected eloquence of a prophet, led the advance. At dawn on August 31, in a torrential downpour, the 11th Armored Division entered Amiens, rousing from sleep Frenchmen who had gone to bed under the Nazi occupation and who erupted into the streets in their nightclothes to applaud the liberating Allies.

Of the four bridges crossing the Somme at that point, three were delivered intact to the British Armed forces by the

French Resistance. At the headquarters of the German Seventh Army, less than 1500 meters from the spearheading Allied tanks, the commander hurriedly turned over his job to his second and attempted to escape in a Volkswagen, still clad in very elegant pajamas. He was captured and taken prisoner.

On September 2, the Guards Armored Division, moving up the east flank of the 11th Armored, reached the Belgian-French frontier southeast of Lille. Farther to the east, two American tank divisions arrived in Belgium, cutting off the road from Lille to Mens. Three Allied Army corps—one British, two American—lined up from the frontier to Brussels.

On the afternoon of September 3, 1944, the Guards Armored entered a Brussels delirious with joy. The next evening, Antwerp was liberated, but German troops still held both sides of the Scheldt Estuary, leading to the port. Nevertheless, the German 15th Army was isolated, apparently cut off, in Flanders and the 7th was in flight.

But despite these successes, German resistance elsewhere was strengthening. On the Moselle, opposite Patton's forces, the 3rd and 15th Grenadier Panthers were back from Italy and fighting next to two SS brigades brought from Germany. On September 3, 1944 (the day after a conference at Chartres attended by General Omar Bradley, Patton and Eisenhower) Hitler, hoping to slow down the Allied northern advance, decided to counterattack Patton's Third Army and the American flank of Monty's army. This was a useless effort. By the time Model, Hitler's commander-in-chief in the West front, received this order, the British were already marching on Brussels.

On September 4, there was a change in the German high command. Old Field Marshal Gerd von Rundstedt was given back the command of the West front which he had lost on July 2, because he failed to drive the Allies off the Normandy beaches. His replacement had been Field Marshal Gunther von Kluge who, in turn, had been replaced by Model, when von Kluge was implicated in the abortive attempt to assassinate Hitler on July 20.

Model was now freed for more active command and took over Army Group B in Belgium and Holland. His superiors were counting on him to hold a front extending from Switzerland to the North Sea—about 600 kilometers (roughly 370 miles)—with only twenty-five divisions. He hastened to dispel them of this illusion. In a message dated September 4, addressed to operations chief Colonel General Alfred Jodel, he asked for twenty-five fresh divisions in support, plus an armored reserve of five—preferably six—divisions. Even then he only planned on holding Antwerp—"the rampart of the West"—and warned that if he did not receive these reinforcements "the door of northwest Germany would remain open."

As these demands conflicted badly with what was possible at the moment, the German High Command satisfied itself by giving him the nucleus of the First Parachute Army, formed on September 4 (under Student)—30,000 men of the Luftwaffe who, due to lack of equipment, were going to fight on foot; six brigades of 10,000 men each of *Volksgrenadier* formed by Gestapo chief Heinrich Himmler, who had to scrape the bottom of the manpower barrel to put them together; two infantry divisions; a brigade of Dutch SS; the garrisons of the "military region of the Netherlands" and, to crown everything, deep sea divers!

The Siegfried Line at this time existed in name only: it was unmanned and had been stripped of its guns. Between the German 15th and 7th Armies there was a beach seventy-five kilometers wide. The door to northwest Germany was, therefor, "gaping on the Albert Canal."

On September 8, the Allied line on the river Meuse jumped. Liege was liberated. In the Ardennes, American troops were nearing Bastogne. Further north, on the afternoon of September 10, the British Horse Guards discovered an opening between Bourg-Leopold and Hechtel; the Grenadiers and the Irish Guards that night reached the British-Dutch frontier near Neerpelt, future jump-off point for the vast air-ground offensive Montgomery was planning.

The British commander had not given up his dream of a backdoor northern thrust into Germany that would let him win the war before another winter set in. Now, on September 10, he met with Eisenhower again, in a plane at Brussels' airport, and presented his latest plan.

It called for the use of the First Allied Airborne Army, formed in August, in England, under the command of U.S. General Lewis Brereton. The paratroopers would be dropped behind enemy lines, in Holland, to "unroll like a carpet" and open the way for his Second Army ground forces, at the same time cutting off the enemy's retreat. Mainly, he was counting on the paratroopers to capture and hold the strategic bridges between the Belgian-Dutch frontier and the Lower Rhine. With the bridges secured, he could throw his Second Army into the hole, cross the Rhine, shut the Siegfried Line—which stopped to the north of Aix-la-Chapelle—and take up position on the edge of the North German plain—between Arnhem and Zivolle—from where he could launch his troops against the Ruhr.

While Eisenhower liked the idea of an airborne assault, he felt the final objective should be more modest: "to reach beyond the Western enemy frontier reasonable positions allowing for regrouping and organizing the technical support of a future advance into Germany."

In short, he approved the plan but with reservations. Once again, Montgomery did not get everything he asked for. He was to get even less than he thought.

On September 15, Eisenhower sent a message to Montgomery and Bradley which he concluded by saying: "We will soon occupy the Ruhr, the Saar and the Frankfurt region."

He was so certain of it that he refused to divert to Montgomery's defensive flank eight divisions of the American First Army which General Patton claimed for himself. General Miles C. Dempsey, commanding the British Second Army, therefore saw himself forced to bring up the VIIIth Corps to protect the right of the XXXth Corps. This did not solve the technical problems—and did not prevent Patton from remaining stalled in front of Metz.

Where transport and other supplies were concerned, Montgomery did not get what he asked for either. Eisenhower's orders were evidently not even respected. And Patton diverted fuel Montgomery needed to his own use. When reproached, he cried: "My men can swell out their bellies, but my tanks need fuel to advance!"

So Montgomery, who theoretically had fifty-two divisions at his disposal, could only use three airborne divisions and three divisions of the XXXth Corps to launch his offensive and had to be content with cutting Holland in two with a sabre cut, renouncing at the same time any hope of driving on into the Ruhr. To manage this "cut" with the XXXth Corps, he had to capture and hold a corridor eighty kilometers long and two kilometers wide.

The success of "Operation Market Garden" (Market for the airborne troops, Garden for the ground forces) was dependent, above all, on surprise and at least forty-eight hours of good weather. About the latter, the British Meteorological Office proved to be unduly optimistic.

At the last minute, Montgomery almost cancelled his offensive, but changed his mind when he learned that the British War Office was counting on him to at least secure the V2 rocket launch sites, near The Hague, from which London was being rocket-bombed.

It would be no small matter to "unroll a carpet" for General Horrocks' XXXth Corps, by capturing the bridges over the three great parallel rivers: the Maas, the Waal and the Lower Rhine.

The plan was to drop the 101st Airborne Division (General Maxwell Taylor commanding) between Veghel and Zar to the north of Eindhoven; the 82nd Airborne (Brig. General James M. Gavin) south of Nijmegen, between the Maas and the Waal; and the British First Airborne Division (Maj. General Robert E. Urquhart commanding), reinforced by Major General Stanislau Sosabowski's Polish 1st Parachute Brigade, would drop near the Lower Rhine, west of Arnhem.

Because of the size of the operation, it would take three days to deliver all of the paratroopers, their supplies, vehicles, guns, etc., to their drop areas. This was one of the plan's great weaknesses—and it proved to be disastrous. In spite of the number of aircraft involved—over 4000—there still were not enough to transport everything and everybody at the same time, or even the same day:

Combat Planes			Transport		
Type	US	GB	Unit	Planes	Gliders
Bombers	891	222	1st. D. Brit.	155	358
Fighters	869	371	82nd D. US	482	50
Fighter-bombers	2212	—	101st D. U.S.	436	70
			EM of CA	—	13

In addition, fighter bombers of the 2nd Tactical Air Force

launched 550 sorties against all known Luftwaffe bases on the eve of the attack, to help clear the way for the XXXth Corps.

The big unknown, inconceivable but nevertheless true, was the true strength of the enemy in the drop areas. General Dempsey's Second Army intelligence people signaled activity among German troops in central Holland, as well as military movement by rail in the Arnhem-Nijmegen area. They reported new flak batteries and batteries of 88 mm anti-tank guns. Still, the enemy force was calculated at only six infantry battalions, twenty tanks and twenty-five motorized cannons with twelve 88s.

But reports from the Dutch Resistance warned that unless the Allies moved fast and threw up an impregnable defense wall of men and armor, they were going to find six battalions at Nijmegen and two Panzer divisions concealed in the region from Nijmegen to Arnhem. A telegraphed report to London over clandestine radio stated:

SS Hohenstruff (sic) division along the Ijssel. Detachments observed between Arnhem and Zutphen as well as along the Zutphen-Apeldoorn Road. Fortification works in progress on the Ijssel.

The British 21st Army Group information people pooh-poohed such reports as "defeatest." They dismissed them as "without any foundation"—in particular the reports about SS armor camouflaged in the woods near Arnhem. Twenty-First Group confirmed work on defenses to lengthen the *Reichswald*—using forced labor "consisting of young Dutchmen of twelve"—but added that these defenses were not serious, nothing to take much notice of.

But, more cautious, a SHAEF informations officer and an officer of the 21st Army Group declared that they thought that they recognized in the armored divisions described by the Resistance the 9th (Hohenstaufen) and 10th (Frundsberg) armored divisions of II *SS Panzer Korps* which had abandoned Normandy to escape annihilation. Unfortunately, the pair were treated as dreamers.

In the days before D Day, Operations Market Garden intelligence information officers of the First Airborne Army struggled with all of the often contradictory information put at their disposal to get an accurate picture of the German

forces in the Low Countries. At last they delivered their con-
clusions:

The paratroopers must expect to meet a pretty strong concentration of flack, a brigade consisting of about 3,000 men,
some tanks, few heavy weapons. Thus they struck off the list
20,000 men with their armor located by the Resistance in the
Hengolo-Bicholt-Cleves district, the armored group which was
returning to Germany and which Bittrich had stopped on the
way; the two Panzer SS divisions on the Ijssel path and in the
Arnhem-Zutphen-Apeldoon region. These were the men the
Allied assault troops would have to fight, skillfully concealed
in the villages east of Arnhem, in the woods and in the fields,
along the roads, under trees and camouflage net; men equipped
with Panther and Super-Tiger tanks, mobile 88s and *Jugd-
panther* anti-tank guns (88s set up on the undercarriages of
Panther tanks).

As if that weren't bad enough, Operation Market Garden
had hardly begun when a glider crashed north of General
Student's HQ at Vught. A member of the patrol which
searched the dead (there were no survivors) found some
documents on an American officer which he handed over to
his sergeant. A few hours later, Kurt Student was looking at
the complete dossier on Market Garden.

He immediately alerted the Luftwaffe. Then, after closer
study, he concluded that if Arnhem fell into the hands of the
Allied paratroopers and if the XXXth Corps succeeded in
joining them, the invasion of Germany would no longer be in
doubt.

So, the curtain lifted on the battle for Arnhem—as we have
seen—on Sunday, September 17, 1944, at 1330 hours, when
the first Allied paratroopers were released practically on Karl
Student's head and almost in Field Marshal Model's lap.

The British 1st Airborne Division made an uneventful
arrival to the west of Arnhem, losing only 38 gliders out of
358 and those by mistake. The 1st Airlanding Brigade, under
Brigadier Philip Hicks, took up positions around the drop
zone to cover the men dropping after them. The First Parachute Brigade, Brigadier Gerald Lathbury commanding,
moved out toward Arnhem.

The Dutch, at first, did not understand what was happening.

They were so used to Allied planes flying over to hit targets inside Germany that they ignored the air armada until, against the soft blue sky, they saw hundreds of parachutes unfold—pink, blue, brilliant yellow, red. A majestic celestial regatta unfolding wave upon wave.

"The Allies are coming!" they cried as the small, vulnerable, swaying puppets dropped to the moor, in the middle of heather and sand. From houses furthest away from the drops, cyclists started out. The whole countryside hummed. People excitedly showed each other the sky. Nervous German occupation officers insisted—in vain—that the Dutch go home.

The Resistance went to work. Silent, discreet, they mingled with the excited crowds, observed the bewildered German troops. Distinguished by orange arm bands, they came out of the shadows at designated drop zones, "reception committees" retrieving containers of supplies and arms, piling them on farm carts and taking them to designated "depots."

Thus a farmer from the Arnhem area, William van Vhiet, found himself at the end of a day and night of work in possession of fifty-three tons of war material that, to his startled surprise, only seven or eight men were left to guard! When he protested, an English officer told him bluntly that he knew what he was doing. The Germans, he said, were on the run. Besides, there were few of them without tanks or heavy weapons.

It took all the horror of battle to prove to the English that the Dutch Resistance knew what it was talking about when it sent London the German battle order in the Low Countries.

Elsewhere that first day, September 17, Operation Market Garden was on schedule. At 1430 hours, an hour after the paratroopers were dropped, General Horrocks launched his XXX Corps up the narrow white band of the only road leading to Eindhoven which was open to him. Leading off was a squadron of tanks, followed by two squadrons of tanks carrying infantry, then by the rest of the Guards.

Ten minutes before the lead tanks moved out, artillery laid down a barrage eight kilometers deep and one and a half kilometers wide. Then the TAF planes went in to bomb suspected enemy emplacements. When the tanks of the Irish Guards, which were opening the way, started up the road, an armored half-track equipped with radio-telephone went with them to call in the planes as needed.

The infantry-carrying tanks followed. The men jumped down and deployed, clearing the enemy out of the woods that came down to the road on both sides. They took a number of prisoners, whom they didn't have time to send to the rear, so they invited them to join them on the tanks.

The captured Germans, stupified, were at first delighted to be so cordially received. They grabbed the Spam, the tea and cigarettes they were offered. But then common sense returned and they realized they were now targets for their own artillery —which they found extremely unpleasant. Hastily, they indicated the location of artillery batteries and camouflaged machine-gun nests so their new-found friends could silence them.

By the end of the day, the Irish Guards had reached Valkenswaards, eight kilometers from Eindhoven. Two tank battalions, one infantry battalion, 400 cannon and 100 TAF planes had successfully opened the way for the rest of the XXXth Corps. The next day, September 18, the Guards and the 101st Airborne linked up at Eindhoven. Twelve hours later, they entered Nijmegen, capturing the bridge at Zon on the way.

In their area, the 82nd Division, under General Gavin, seized the bridge over the Maas at Grave, skirted the *Reichswald* and headed north toward the Waal and the bridge at Nijmegen.

But at Arnhem things had taken a far more dramatic turn . . .

The first drop, Sunday, September 17, was not as uneventful as first supposed. Though only a few gliders had been lost, these turned out to be carrying the heavy armor and transport vehicles. This left the Division without adequate mobility and protection. It was also without radio communication. The radios had arrived in such bad condition it was impossible to use them.

The Division tried borrowing the radios of BBC correspondents accompanying them, but their signal was drowned out by the overpowering signal of a nearby German radio station. A radio-equipped Phantom field-intelligence unit was no better help.

By now the Division was grimly aware that the woods surrounding its landing area were a death trap. Hidden in the
brush, the Germans waited for the next wave of troop carriers
and gliders. They waited until the men jumped and the gliders
were released, then they opened fire on their defenseless targets. But the drops continued, because it was essential to get
equipment and reinforcements to the troops already on the
ground.

Trapped, not being able to change their ground, the Allies
concentrated their fire on the edge of the woods hiding the
Germans. Hidden under the trees in the nearby villages and
towns, Panther and Tiger tanks moved out to attack the
British, then returned to their bases to be tended by their
maintenance crews. Thus whole towns became gigantic open-
air garages.

Night and day, surrounded by the noise of machine guns,
mortars and thundering tank guns, the British struggled to
reach the bridge at Arnhem, to cross it and hold the access.
They transformed their road into a bloody route strewn with
corpses, but they fought on grimly, hoping to hold out until
Horrocks' XXX Corps could reach them.

Between Oosterbeek and Arnhem, they fought; around and
in the Saint Elizabeth Hospital, a spread-out building surrounded by a low wall which the Germans had managed to
turn into a small fort. After three vain tries, the British managed to infiltrate the place, fighting among the sick, the doctors and nurses, the treatment wagons, on top of occupied beds.

In the city—in Arnhem—the battle was fought from street
to street, block to block, house to house. Everywhere there
was the sound of battle—bombs exploding, machine guns chat-
tering, bazookas exploding—and the stink of blood and death.
Fires broke out all over the city.

The townspeople, resigned, took cover in the cellars. Here
they cared for the wounded, fed those who were still fighting,
comforted those who could not go on. They served as messengers, liaison agents, moving back and forth under the crossfire.
Some chose to wear the orange armband of the Resistance, and
fifty were captured and shot before the eyes of the 1st Division
commander, General Urquhart, who was himself trapped for
a time inside the beleaguered city.

It could not go on forever. The First British Parachute
Division must be relieved, or it was doomed . . .

Relief was on the way but it, too, ran into unexpected
trouble. On Thursday, Septembed 21, D-day plus four, the
XXX Corps infantry reached Nijmegen and relieved the Irish
Guards who moved out quickly to close the fifteen kilometer
gap which separated them from Arnhem. But the way was
blocked—by Bittrich's Supertigers and Panthers, who attacked repeatedly under the protection of 500 Luftwaffe
fighters.

On Friday, September 22, General Horrocks—whose original orders called for pushing on to the Zuiderzee—decided
to concentrate all his efforts instead on bringing help to the
besieged troops at Arnhem who, gathered into an ever-shrink-
ing perimeter on the wrong bank of the Lower Rhine, were
almost at the end of their strength. But by Sunday it was evi-
dent that there was no hope of reaching them in time. "The
Red Devils" had lost the round.

On the night of September 25, their retreat began. Under
cover of darkness, in an heroic effort, General Urquhart managed to get 2400 of his men back to safety across the river.
The rest of the 10,000 men who took part in the attack on
Arnhem were dead, wounded, prisoners of war, or missing.

At dawn on Tuesday, September 26, the noise of battle
subsided. A young Dutchwoman came out of the cellar at
Oosterbeek where she had been hiding for six days. At first
she recognized nothing about the surrealistic landscape which
surrounded her and was reflected in the pool of water in the
bottom of a German helmet. Roofs and walls had crumbled
into one heap; it was a nightmare. The light of day seemed
to have a strange intensity. A light breeze blew across the
ruins. An apocalyptic silence reigned, like the silence of Hiro-
shima after the explosion of the A-bomb.

Those, like Churchill, who claimed later that Arnhem had
been ninety percent successful never saw the ruin, the thousands of dead and injured that were its price. They could only
have been thinking of covering up a catastrophe for which
they felt at least partly responsible.

Who *was* responsible? Some tried to make Field Marshal

Montgomery shoulder all the blame. Eisenhower, for instance, wrote that he hoped Monty "would at least understand his mistake." But the British field marshal was not so easily intimidated. In his memoirs, he declares that Arnhem would have been completely successful if Eisenhower had known how to make a decision and stick to it. Had Operation Market Garden been provided with sufficient logistical support, he argues, it would have succeeded and the war would have been shortened by eight months, an objective which should have been worth the risk. It would have spared the Dutch another year of Nazi occupation—of famine, torture, forced labor and death.

Operation Market Garden was a disaster. Only at Eindhoven and Nijmegen did the British Second Army Infantry succeed in linking up with the "carpet laying" paratroopers.

At Eindhoven, the model Phillips plant, which supplied Germany with most of its electricity had been liberated intact by the airborne troops. Everybody celebrated with the U.S. paratroopers. The streets were dressed with orange decorations. The Phillips workers and their families frantically searched for anything that would make a noise: whistles, tambourines, wooden rattles. They threw back their heads and joyfully sang religious hymns—which they sometimes interrupted with the national anthem.

"Eindhoven," noted a war correspondent, "as bright as a new penny, celebrated its liberation as though it were Christmas Day."

Then at 1700 hours on the 21st of September, a rumor began to spread through the town: "The Germans are returning." Suddenly the streets were empty. One could hear doors shutting, then silence. All activity was centered at the Phillips complex, the military headquarters of the Resistance.

A doctor fourteen kilometers north of Eindhoven phoned to signal that six German tanks were heading towards the town. A railwayman warned of the approach of four Panthers. Other tanks were arriving from the east. A column of German infantry had been spotted.

The British Guard, pushing their advantage, had already left the town when, at dusk on September 21, the Luftwaffe arrived with its flares. The flares were unnecessary, because they were going to bomb a target the pilots knew well.

One wing of the Phillips plant burst into flames. Six shelled trucks blew up one after the other, forming a moving sheet of fire whose flames touched a cache of light arms and ammunition and set it off like an endless string of firecrackers.

From the cellars where the Dutch had taken shelter rose the obstinate strains of a hymn. It began to rain then, quietly, on the fields north of Eindhoven where hundreds of multi-colored parachutes lay among the brilliant white streaks of gliders—large, clumsy, headless, pitiful abandoned beasts.

Returning to the offensive, the Germans now attempted to cut off an Allied column stretching fifty kilometers—right back to Belgium. General Horrocks fought them off each time with his armor. The paratroopers forded the river at Nijmegen, despite a strong eight-knot current that spun their light boats around like dancers. The bridge was taken and held, but icy mud pinned down the Allied tanks. Arnhem was decidedly far away.

Veghl, Eindhoven, Nijmegen on its rock peak, Arnhem—once the favorite residence of traders returning from the Indies—all the little towns in the most picturesque region of Holland were devastated by war. But from the ruins their inhabitants emerged, unconquerable, to aid the Allied wounded, help with supplies, communications.

The Nazis held the official postal system but another had always functioned without their knowledge. The power company in Gelderland Province had installed a switchboard at its center in Arnhem which connected with all the militia in towns wherever the company had an office. These installations had functioned always for the greatest convenience of the Resistance and the Allies.

On September 27, in reprisal against the recalcitrant Dutch population, the Germans ordered Arnhem's 100,000 inhabitants evacuated. They considered evacuating the entire Gelderland Province but gave up the idea because the resultant chaos would have made Model's military situation impossible. Oosterbeek and the other towns west of Arnhem suffered the same fate: evacuation within twenty-four hours.

During that winter of cold, famine and destitution, their exiled populations overran the rest of Holland, begging for shelter and food, the young, the sick, the old, taking refuge where they could—in the forests most of the time—until

misery threw them on the roads again, only to die of exposure
or starvation or by machine-gun from the RAF when they
mingled with the movements of German troops.

In the deserted cities, the looters took over. Cologne, Bonn,
Mannheim and Dusseldorf received truck and train cars full
of goods—some useful, some bizarre: cases of curtain rings,
truncks of tire jacks, drills, hairdressers' scissors, pocket knives.
There were grab-bag bundles of false teeth, croquet balls,
embroidery hoops, hammers, hair tonic, horse shoes—nothing
was overlooked.

The Allied advance had been checked. The German occupation continued in the rest of the country, but the German
"order" had been irreparably beaten. The chaos was un-
imaginable. Control was impossible. The idea of verification of
identity, for instance, suddenly seemed mad. Nothing made
any sense in that devastated, unyielding hostile countryside . . .
the bitter fruit of Arnhem, the disaster Christiaan Lindemans
would suffer for along with his homeless countrymen who had
touched the hand of liberty only to have it snatched away.

CHAPTER THREE

Antwerp was liberated on September 4, 1944, and Christiaan Lindemans could legitimately say, "I was there."

He was there to help the Resistance "clean up" the harbor installations. Antwerp was an important objective for SHAEF, because three months after "Overlord" (the invasion of Normandy) supplies for Eisenhower's armies, as well as supplies for the civilians in the liberated areas, could still come in only through the port of Cherbourg. But liberating Antwerp and its port without paralyzing it would not be easy.

The town—even the suburbs—and its harbor installations were all grouped on the east bank of the Scheldt, which was 300 to 500 meters wide at that point. Approaching their objective from the west, the Allies would find one tunnel for pedestrians and one tunnel by which vehicles could cross the river. They were side by side and both could be easily obstructed. Coming from the south, the Allies would have to cross the Rupel, a marshy river 125 meters wide, and the Willebrock Canal, 40 meters wide, with a bridge to secure at Bron, on the Brussels-Antwerp-Walen-Duffel-Lierre *autostrada*.

Thanks to the Belgian Resistance, a route was agreed upon with SHAEF, marked out by guides and cleared of German mines. On September 3, the regional Resistance leader made contact with the British at Engheim, and with the SOE (Special Operations Executive) and the Belgian secret army at Brussels. On September 4, at 1030 hours, access to Antwerp was clear.

They fought successively on the southern outskirts of the city, on the ancient ramparts, from the Place de Meir as far as the end of the Rue Rouge, where the tanks of the Guards met the German troops who were fleeing the city in indescribable confusion.

Thus, on the evening of September 4, the town properly recovered its independence. Flowers were piled high on the liberators' tanks. Alternately laughing and crying, the people offered the English all the provisions they had left—cigarettes, wine, beer, biscuits, pork—crying: "Thank you! Thank you!" In their turrets, the tank crews did not know if they were going to burst into laughter or burst into tears.

All this emotion during the night and days of September 4 and 5, plus the seizure of the main buildings, the Bonaparte Lock, the Royers Lock, the Strasbourg Bridge, the Albert Dock, the Leopold Dock and the Albert Canal, had the people believing that the Allies had been completely successful.

The Germans had decided not to defend Antwerp, but they intended to render the port unserviceable for a long time. Fortified on the northern bank of the Scheldt, they held on fiercely to one part of the Albert Canal, the Kruischam, the Lutchtbal and other docks. In Merksem they had taken up a firm position and fought desperately. It was what the Allies had feared and why Christiaan Lindemans and others in his Resistance group had received the order to infiltrate the harbor area and clean it out without too much material damage, if possible.

The SHAEF battle plans for Antwerp, notably the coordination of the Allied troops' action with the missions of the Resistance, had been made with particular care—thanks to close cooperation between SHAEF, the Belgian government in exile and the Belgian Resistance military authorities.

The action was divided into three phases, each having a

code name, each to be launched when an agreed-on "personal message" incorporating the code was read over the BBC:

Phase 1 called for the dislocation of German rail traffic. The code sentence was: "Solomon has put on his large clogs."

Phase 2 called for the harrassment of enemy troops and the sabotage of enemy telephone communications. Code sentence: "The yellow daffodil is in flower."

Phase 3 called for the start of an open fight. Code sentence: "The foliage on the trees hides the old mill from us."

These orders were given on June 1, June 8 and September 1, 1944, respectively. The first two messages did not concern Christiaan Lindemans directly, but the last one did, so he knew the Resistance battle plans and the code messages that would be used.

He could have furnished the Germans with essential information for which the Abwehr had been searching for over a year. In fact, the first-phase code sentence—"Solomon has put on his large clogs"—could only indicate that the Allies were on the verge of invading mainland Europe. Certainly Colonel Giskes would have grasped its meaning immediately.

Yet, Giskes himself admitted—during interrogation by the Allies after the war and in his memoirs—that Christiaan had deceived him by not giving him the slightest indication concerning the Normandy landings.

Strange behavior for a man who was soon to stand accused of treason!

On September 1, 1944, Christiaan knew he had to reach his action station in Antwerp. There he fought heroically for three days. Then, on the evening of September 4, the Resistants' ammunition started running out.

Requests for more were denied. The Allies could no longer supply the volunteers. They had to keep what they had for what they described as a "grand offensive," still being studied, but which could render the finishing stroke to the Germans. So the battle for the large part became sporadic, with the Germans fortifying themselves more and more solidly in the docks. Actually, the failure of Market Garden made it necessary to clean out the docks at Antwerp islet by islet, which took until November 8, 1944.

It was then that Christiaan decided to change his seat of

war. The prolonged guerrilla warfare which the Germans imposed bored him. Besides, he was Dutch and it was his country which would be free tomorrow!

To understand his state of mind, one must understand Tuesday, September 5, 1944, mad Tuesday—*dolle dinsdag* as they said in the Low Countries. The British tanks seemed to throw themselves forward, never stopping until they reached the Dutch border. The Dutch, thinking they were on the brink of liberty, lost their heads with joy. The Germans, thinking they were about to be overrun, flung themselves on the roads, forming a stream of retreating humanity which soon became a raging torrent.

The delirious Dutch population cried: "This time, it's the end!" Naturally, the echoes of *dolle dinsdag* reached Belgium. After almost five years of living in hell, Christiaan had only one idea in his head: to go home, join his own people.

This was how he happened to find himself face to face with a detachment of Phantoms—British advance units for "irregular" reconnaissance work. This group, which had entered Antwerp on the heels of the guards, was called the "Buccaneers" and was commanded by twenty-four-year-old Captain Peter Baker.

A writer, poet and editor who had been bored with his assignment to the War Office, Baker had been transferred in 1942 to the very special Phantom units then being formed. He served in North Africa, Sicily and Italy before landing in Normandy with the Irish Guards, his original corps.

Theoretically, a detachment of Phantoms consisted of two officers, two second officers and troops, briefed on the movements of the Resistance, serving—among other things—as liaison between the irregular and regular fighting forces. They had their own transport and their own radio transmitters. They received their orders straight from their commander, General Airey Neave, a master of irregular operations, based in Paris since August 23, 1944.

At Antwerp, on September 5, 1944, Peter Baker—like Christiaan Lindemans—was anxious to get moving again. But the Guards had set out leaving him behind, simply because he could not find any transport!

His right hand, Gunner Mackenzie, was at his wit's end. Even Charles Muller, attached to the Baker mission since the liberation of Paris, on orders of the French Army Minister, "for the length of the Phantom mission's stay in France" and who had elected to stay with them right into Belgium because his new friends conducted a type of war which amused him, had no solution.

That was the situation when suddenly there materialized, in front of Captain Baker, a young giant about his own age toting a machine gun and draped with ammo belts, grenades and small arms. Unshaven, covered with oil, wearing a British paratrooper's outfit embellished with a captain's stars, exhausted but delighted, Christiaan Lindemans introduced himself—in his usual modest way: "The liberator of Antwerp—that's me!"

Baker took this amazing pronouncement in his usual cool stride. "I command a group called the 'Buccaneers,'" he said, introducing himself. "And if you can find us a means of transport, I would be really most grateful."

Krist, the nickname by which Baker was to remember Christiaan Lindemans, smiled with satisfaction. The Buccaneers did not look like choir boys exactly, yet they needed him—King Kong—to find them a car. Well, he would requisition one for them. Nothing could be easier!

In fact, a few hours later he delivered a sumptuous Cadillac, complete with chauffeur, announcing to Baker: "Old man, have confidence in me. She works . . . I know. As a civilian, I worked in a garage."

We know very little, apart from this, about that first meeting between the two. It is a shame, for it must have been quite a sight.

Thin, distinguished, a bit vague, a bit fragile, the young Englishman had enormous charm. He was friendly, knew how to pass unnoticed, said very little about his exploits and his career with the Irish Guards. He was happy to listen, and had a good sense of humor.

Christiaan Lindemans, by contrast, was taller by at least a foot and solidly built. He had the gift of gab of the Rotterdam child and fantastic nerve. An ex-boxer, a traffic accident had left him with a slight limp and a deformed hand. The son of a garage owner, born into a most respectable family—lower middle-class and conformist—he had become a hero of the Dutch Resistance, a legendary figure known from the

Granigue to Spain. He did not need much urging to start boasting.

He loved women, noise, drink and a good fight. He certainly did not pass unnoticed—except when a mission demanded it. He usually chose to wear a leather jacket. He had blue eyes, a pale complexion, almost blond hair. "He was not really blond, but he gave the impression of being so because he was so pale," Captain Kas de Graff, who worked with him in the Resistance, once described him.

At ease, Christiaan had a detached expression, childlike and a little surprised. But he sometimes got into uncontrollable rages which were very frightening.

At the moment, he was overjoyed at having found a car for his new friends.

He accompanied them to Bourg-Leopold, giving Baker information he needed to accomplish his mission. Nobody knew the Dutch and Belgian networks as well as Krist. But, while the Buccaneers went on about their business, the chauffeur disappeared with the Cadillac!

"Of no importance," Krist assured them. "We will find another, but Charles must come with me. Two officers are better than one."

Twenty-four hours later, the pair returned, driving the Cadillac but minus the chauffeur.

"Krist doesn't think we really need the chauffeur—that we're better off without him," Charles explained.

The Phantoms moved on to Hechtel. The armoured Guards reached the Milhelmine Canal at Groove-Barriere where Captain Baker began recruiting new troops. Thirty-six Russians and twenty-six Frenchmen suddenly appeared from nowhere.

"Now. . . ," Baker turned to Krist, "my orders are to wait for the Second Army to pass on to the offensive against Valkenswaard and Eindhoven. But the Eindhoven resistants need to be warned first. Krist, could you do this for me?"

Christiaan nooded and Baker continued: "You must cross our lines and those of the Germans to get to Eindhoven. You will have to warn the Resistance to be alert, but to wait. They will soon receive arms and orders. Also, we know they are hiding escaped Allied prisoners. You must tell them to keep these people with them—not to attempt to get them across the lines. Is it possible?"

Of course it was possible. And it wouldn't be the first time Christiaan had crossed frontiers and battlelines. Under the occupation, he had traveled a lot—with false papers, real papers or no papers at all, depending on the case. He had been to Sweden, France, even as far as the Pyrenees.

"Is it urgent, your message? When must it arrive at Eindhoven?" was all he asked.

"Let's say before September 15," Baker replied without hesitation.

Now Christiaan knew everything about Operation Market Garden except, perhaps, its code name. He knew it was planned for after September 15. He knew basically what it consisted of, having heard the English say: "When we advance, we will find in front of us a carpet of paratroopers to open the way."

On their side, his friends in the Dutch Resistance had often told him: "It's not worth getting killed in Holland. When Monty launches his offensive, the Nazis will flee, having had enough. Holland will be liberated by the parachutists who will land on the bridges to force the way."

Krist had a premonition, and took leave of his new friends reluctantly. Baker promised that they would "find each other at Eindhoven," but Krist was not at all convinced.

Suddenly his expression lighted up with mischief. "You know," he told Baker, "with your car, your glasses, your uniform, you look like our Prince Bernhard. I'd love to see the Dutch cheer you!"

"I've been mistaken for Monty and managed to carry it off," Baker admitted nonchalantly.

"That's not at all the same," Krist told him. "After all, you and Monty talk the same language. Can you imagine the Prince addressing his people in English?"

"So? What would you do in my place?" asked Baker, caught up in the spirit of the thing.

Krist demonstrated. "Move your hand graciously. Repeat: 'Leve Holland . . . Danke wel . . . and do not loiter! Your people are quite capable of asking you to stop and chat."

Baker was to follow this excellent advice at Valkenswaard and at Aalst—on the road to Eindhoven—where he had to take refuge with the PC of the Irish Guards to escape the general enthusiasm.

Christiaan would have to use a more discreet method to get back to Holland, but not right away. Instead, he retraced his steps and headed for Brussels, telling himself he deserved a few days off. Besides, he had to speak to his superiors—tell them about his new contact—before taking the next step in the dangerous game he had agreed to play for them.

A few days later, Christiaan left for Holland. By September 14, he had reached Vught, the HQ of Kurt Student, given the password Colonel Giskes had provided him with, and was sent on to Dreibergen and Major Kiesewetter of the Abwehr.

He had to undergo an interminable interrogation in front of a group of officers in Kiesewetter's office. Questions were fired at him, which he answered, but more and more vaguely.

When would the British Second Army move off? What units would support it on the guard flank? What route would they take? What was the final objective? Where would the paratroopers jump? Then came detailed questions on the units which Christiaan could have seen in Belgium, questions about the troops' morale and their equipment.

Hours passed. Cigarettes accumulated in the ashtrays. Orderlies brought beer, wine and sandwiches. Finally, Major Kiesewetter stretched himself and said:

"I think that is all. A car will drive you to the Eindhoven area so you can meet the Resistance. . . ."

Then he gave him a new mission to fulfill and told him to return to Dreibergen within three days.

Christiaan Lindemans would not present himself . . .

What happened next and exactly when is not clear. But about the time Colonel Giskes must have been congratulating himself on how his confidence in "C.C." had paid off, in Brussels, at the headquarters of Prince Bernhard (commander in chief of all Dutch forces, including the Resistance "irregulars") a message was being prepared destined for Eindhoven:

"From the headquarters of the Dutch forces in Belgium," it began. "A man known as Lindemans is on his way to join you. Treat him with extreme prudence. Pass over to him the formal order to rejoin this headquarters as quickly as possible. He will see that he has been entrusted with an urgent mission. Lindemans knows personally the officer who awaits him."

Yes, Christiaan knew the officer who summoned him— Captain Kas de Graf. He should have: he once saved the man's life.

The message concluded with: "Please acknowledge." Its recipient, a young police officer working for the Resistance named Kooy, replied at once:

"Your communication . . . very surprising. Instructions understood. Will nevertheless be carried out to the letter."

Now destiny was on the march. Christiaan Lindemans had begun the last round. The liberation would not bring him what he expected.

On September 16, a German *Wehrmacht* car drove him to the outskirts of Eindhoven. Now Christiaan was in a hurry. It was important that he find his friends in the network and pass on the instructions he had received from Baker. There was little time; the next day the paratroopers would jump on the Low Countries.

Night fell. Christiaan Lindemans walked the back roads toward the men who were waiting for him—toward a policeman named Kooy.

Kooy received him awkwardly. Hastily he passed on to him the order received from the Prince's headquarters, as if he wanted to be quickly rid of the job.

The Resistance—Christiaan's friends—had read and reread the message from Brussels, shaking their heads, wellaware of what it meant. Was it possible. . . ? There had been other traitors, of course, but surely . . . Christiaan Lindemans? They had worked with him, shared so many dangers with him . . . But, if Headquarters said . . .

The leader of the partisans remarked that "those who believe there is no smoke without fire, those who prefer not to know, who repeat that an order is an order, those people are not asked to judge, but to execute."

The Prince wanted Lindemans to be sent back to his headquarters, but would he go? Blind discipline was not at all his style. To make certain that he would get there, he would have to be accompanied, but this was not the time to be deprived of a man. Great events were about to begin. Everyone would be needed at Eindhoven.'

A new plan was formed. Instead of sending Christiaan back to Brussels, he was to be put where he could do no harm. He would be immobilized, to be sent off on his errand later.

A little group surrounded Christiaan, took him where, he was told, an important rendezvous was to be held. He was told to descend into a coal cellar . . . for security measures.

Unsuspecting, he did as he was told, his friends standing aside to let him pass—friends he trusted so well that he entered the cellar alone. He turned around. Too late! Already the door was shut.

He remained alone, in the dark, while outside the battle for Holland raged . . .

From the bottom of the cellar with a narrow vent for air, Christiaan Lindemans followed the vicissitudes of the fight. He heard the advance bombing of the RAF, then the rumble of the transports, the clanging sound of tanks on the move, the dry cough of gunfire and the characteristic "tac-a-tac, boom tac" of the Tiger cannons.

He knew nothing of the man-in-the-street's joy. The sound of the hymns of his childhood barely reached him. Locked in his prison without glory, biting his knuckles, he waited.

But . . . how could he? How did a man who needed air, space, people put up with such treatment? Could anyone imagine anything more cruel and inhuman? How could he— a sentimental, gentle boy, driven by the need to be loved, admired—control himself? A man who was prey to so many complexes, "who did not belong in elite society" as Bertrand de Jouvenal was to say, "who had not succeeded" and who, as a last indignity, was stabbed in the back by his friends just when they tasted the delicious fruits of victory he had helped them fight for?

How he longed to be outside! How happy he would have been to see the American paratroopers descend from the sky, to see the fields covered with parachutes clumsily hooked onto the fuselages of the gliders.

But time passed, leaving him in the dark. He had to guess everything by sound, like a blind man. He did not know that it was the Irish Guards who joined forces with the 101st Airborne. He did not see them cross the black roads on

September 18. He who would have so happily carried children on his broad shoulders to show them the sight.

And when the soft sound of the rain in the great silence of the night told him that the elements themselves were hostile to the Allies, what did Christiaan Lindemans say to himself, shut in that dark basement?

September 17 . . . 18 . . . slipped slowly by. Christiaan wondered if, as a crowning irony, it might be the Germans who would pull him out of his hole. It was raining harder, and if the Allies had to fight bogged down in the mud, the Nazis would surely make the most of it and counterattack in full, getting their own back at the Dutch who had so joyfully —and prematurely—applauded their liberation.

This indignity, at least, Christiaan was spared. On September 19, when the long martyrdom began at Arnhem, the Buccaneers at last reached Eindhoven.

Charles Muller was with them for a few hours longer, but he had already received an order from the French Minister that he return to Paris at once or be considered a deserter. The Phantoms were waiting for orders from General Neave, who was in Brussels now.

They made themselves comfortable. Captain Baker found himself a liaison officer, Andre Koch, librarian at the University of Leyde.

Leo Hookens, son of a politician, himself a baker, patriot, sabotage expert and arms collector, also offered his services. He was in possession of three shotguns, two automatic pistols, two tommy guns, two machine guns, an American colt, a British mortar and a bazooka.

The sight of Hookens and his arsenal made Baker laugh— and reminded him of Krist. He was suddenly worried because they hadn't yet met. He set to work, questioning, interrogating. All the Buccaneers questioned, and finally they learned the truth. Baker shrugged his shoulders. A stupid mistake, naturally. He intervened—to the great relief of Kooy. Half indignant, half laughing, it was Peter Baker who, on September 19, finally let Krist out of the cellar.

How did the two find each other again? What did they say? Impossible to know; Peter Baker is silent on the subject. But they must have discussed Arnhem, perhaps criticized the operation.

They could not fail to see that Operation Market Garden was not working out too well. They knew that the drops had taken place too far from the bridge at Arnhem; that it had been raining steadily since D-Day plus 1; that Willy Bittrich had suddenly revealed more armor that anyone thought he had.

Peter Baker must have thought about the Phantom unit trapped in the perimeter at Arnhem, sending out anguished appeals from the paratroopers. Christiaan may have wondered who could have alerted Bittrich so far in advance?

But they must have mainly talked about the future. Once more, Christiaan had to leave the Buccaneers. Before Airey Neave arrived to inspect them, he explained to them how they could cross the treacherous, icy water of the Maas and the Waal, right under the Germans' noses.

"Will you wait for me? You promise to wait?" Krist kept asking Peter. "We will do things together."

"I will be delighted . . . if you come back. But perhaps the Prince will want to keep you near him," Baker must surely have answered, or something like it.

Their disjointed conversation hid their anguish and the difficulty of farewell. Christiaan made things easier by swaggering, as usual, saying that of course he would return, for he always came back. After all, he was the great "King Kong."

Somewhere around September 22, Christiaan Lindemans took the road for Belgium. He disappeared into the night, a massive, solitary figure walking toward the unknown. The clouds hanging over him, the misunderstandings, would they clear up? He thought they would. He told himself that he was the strongest, the cleverest, the bravest of men. Surely at the Prince's headquarters his true worth would be recognized.

In fact, they recognized him straight away. He arrived in the middle of a celebration. The Prince was introducing himself to his Resistance fighters.

In his old parachute outfit, Christiaan Lindemans kept his date with Prince Bernhard. He probably deposited his arms at the door, ran a comb through his rebellious hair.

He felt a bit lost in that crowd. He stood alone until, attracted by his tall build and his manner, English journalists, led by the *Daily Mirror* correspondent who smelled a story, went over to talk to him.

Christiaan was not averse to publicity and was happy to oblige. They laughed a lot, drank a bit, and talked.

Later, at the Prince's headquarters they strongly regretted this. Later, the meeting was denied just as it was denied that Lindemans ever visited the HQ before September 22 or 23. It was said that it never took place, that the journalists had invented it to make a good story. Since the censor was most strict, the correspondents allowed themselves to be muzzled. They did not realize at the time that King Kong was important. They only rated him as being rather colorful filler material.

But at the Prince's headquarters they knew that Christiaan Lindemans would soon become *persona non grata,* and they began to keep their distance.

For Christiaan Lindemans it was the sorry end of the dangerous road he had chosen to walk almost five years before . . .

CHAPTER FOUR

April 9, 1940. . . .

"The Germans attacked Denmark and Norway this morning!"

Sprawled on his back, Christiaan Lindemans turned his head toward the sound of the voice and struggled to get out from under the car he was working on.

"Give me a cigarette," he said to the friend who had just announced the beginning of the Nazis' Western offensive.

The young man did as requested, a bit mortified. He had just heard the news on the radio—all Rotterdam would be talking of nothing else soon—and he had hoped for more of a reaction.

But Christiaan, covered with grease, just sat down calmly on the running-board of the car, looking not at all impressed or surprised. Instead, he gave the car a friendly pat and remarked, "I must get this engine in good shape very quickly. I bet you, the owner will not take long to appear—if what you say is true."

"Naturally it's true," his friend said indignantly. "But I don't see what you're getting at!"

"Because you do not know our local bourgeoisie," Chris-

47

tiaan told him calmly. "They did not want to believe in the war, but now you are going to see them panic! They will load their cars with goods and head for their country houses. They have made a mistake—they have got us into a mess—but you can be sure that they won't think of us for a second!"

"They" for Christiaan were the upper middle-classes who dominated Dutch life and presided over the country's political destiny. "They" were the Cavalier of Geer, for example, who became Prime Minister on August 10, 1939.

"If we are attacked, we will fight," his friend declared passionately.

"With what?" Christiaan asked, exhaling. "What is the re-armament they have talked so much about since 1937? What did it give us? According to what I've read, at the beginning of this year the army had, in all, twenty-six armoured vehicles but no tanks, a few modern planes and about fourteen-hundred pieces of artillery, most of it about sixty years old—a good age for wine but not for combat!"

"You exaggerate!" his friend protested. "That is defeatism. If we have to fight, you know very well that we will withdraw to the Grebbe Line—"

"Exactly!" Christiaan nodded. "And isn't that defeatism? To abandon the north, the east and nearly all the south of the country . . . you call that a defense? We will fight on the Grebbe Line, we will withdraw to the Waterline while waiting for the English or the French—with whom we didn't want to ally ourselves—to come to our aid!"

"Listen, Christiaan," his friend argued, "it's not that bad. I tell you that Hitler has attacked Denmark and Norway and that means he won't come here. I will even bet on it!"

Christiaan looked at him. "And why won't he, may I ask?"

"Because he does not need to attack Holland. The Germans didn't do so in 1914!"

Christiaan shrugged. "In 1914, it was not Hitler. We've already had two alerts—"

"And nothing happened," his friend pointed out. "Look, Krist, it's just as I am telling you. If we remain neutral, mind our own business—"

Christiaan reddened, close to losing his temper. He checked himself, which was not at all in character. But . . . what was the use? All of Holland talked like this idiot. All of Holland was neutral—nervously, stupidly neutral. She was rotten with "National Socialism" (Dutch Nazism), paralyzed by the fear of Communism—which had never represented more than three percent of the voters—and corrupted by the heavy prosperity of the ruling classes.

A few days later, the Prime Minister, responding to pressure, initiated arrests of National Socialists. Christiaan and others noted cynically that he did not arrest Anton Mussert, the head of the Dutch Nazi Party, the *National-Socialistische Beweging*, because he was worried about maintaining good relations with Berlin. On top of this, "to appease" Berlin, he was willing to jail a few Communists to show his hostility toward "all totalitarians!"

Christiaan finished his cigarette and got up to wash his hands. At that moment, his mother called him for lunch.

"Are you staying?" he asked his friend, but the other refused, still put out with him.

At the Lindemans' table that midday, they talked, naturally, about the attack that morning. Norway and Denmark had always been neutral. Why invade them without provocation? Why go towards the north? At any rate, Christiaan's father concluded, it proved how useless it was for the Dutch to behave like ostriches. That was not the way to divert the storm.

Christiaan's oldest brother, who had recently married and taken lodgings near the port but still often came home for lunch, disagreed. He was the most home-loving of the Lindemans' sons, happy to settle down as an office employee.

"If you do not respect your own neutrality," he argued, "how do you expect others to do so?"

Christiaan could not restrain himself. "You're a fool!" he shouted. "Hitler respects nothing. The English know it—they offered to help us and we turned them down! That ass, the Cavalier, didn't want to give Hitler a 'pretext' for violating the neutrality of Holland, as if he needed one! As if he wasn't capable of fabricating out of nothing an excellent reason for invading us! Look what is happening now in Denmark and Norway. We will be caught in the middle with nothing to defend ourselves!"

But his brother shook his head obstinately. "The Prime Minister was right. Neither the English nor the French can stop our being invaded if the Wehrmacht decides to attack us. We saw what happened in Belgium during the last war—victorious but ruined, as our chief accountant was saying just the other day."

Christiaan got up and walked around the room like a bear in a cage. These "bureaucrats" like his brother disgusted him! They had never stood on the docks of Rotterdam and heard the call of unknown, faraway lands. For them there was only their own tight little world.

His mother's eyes followed him sadly. She loved him, of course, but he worried her. She often asked herself—her heart full of anguish—what would happen to this son, a boxer who had abandoned the ring, now a garage mechanic, impatient, rebellious, lost in frustrated dreams of adventure. Only Henk, the youngest of her four sons, admired Christiaan without reservation, following him around like a dog, imitating him, copying his way of dressing, of behaving—even his way of losing his temper.

Krist lost it now . . . again. "It is not a question of being rescued or ruined! Your chief accountant is an idiot! We will be invaded because Hitler couldn't care less about our neutrality. We are too near England for him not to take possession of our coastline. That is geography! Debate will not change anything.

"We will fight alone, because we have rejected the aid of the Allies, and we will not hold out any longer than eight days," he concluded. Henk, his mouth full, nodded agreement with his hero.

"Mainly," added the elder Lindemans, quietly, who for once agreed with this problem son of his, "mainly because of the Fifth Column. We are sold, betrayed from inside."

There was suddenly silence at the table. Madame Lindemans replenished the bread basket with black and white bread, various little rolls and croissants, but her mind was not on the task.

The presence and movement of the notorious "Fifth Column" had monopolized Dutch conversation for months. Not only was the Dutch Nazi party considered an almost open ally of Hitler, but it was believed that all the Germans—*Reichsdentschen*—living in the Low Countries were spies.

At the beginning of November, 1939, the son of a well-known member of the NSB had been stopped at the frontier when he was trying to take a trunk containing two complete Dutch soldiers' uniforms—bought "ready-made" in Amsterdam—a postman's outfit, a policeman's uniform, and a railwayman's outfit across to Germany. At the time, Christiaan had raged, "It is Gleiwitz all over again. Tomorrow the Germans will be here—and who will receive them? The Fifth Column!" At Gleiwitz, a little village on the German-Polish border, German soldiers wearing Polish uniforms had faked an attack on the radio station.

But at lunch, that April 9, Krist's older brother still remained stubbornly unconvinced. "Oh you and your Fifth Column!" he scoffed.

He and others like him soon had to back down. A few days after the German attack on Denmark and Norway, The Hague announced that it had discovered a bulky envelope with the official stamp of the Third Reich addressed to a Doctor Cohrs, in Berlin. It contained fifteen pages crammed with notes, signed by a member of the German embassy in The Hague, and gave the details of new military defenses in the Netherlands.

Even so, the Dutch were still discussing, passionately, the best course to follow when the OKW—*Oberkommando der Werhmacht*, German Armed forces High Command—brutally put an end to all debate.

On May 10, 1940, in beautiful spring weather, the Germans crossed the Dutch border at several points and Luftwaffe planes attacked airfields in the western part of the country. Later that morning, a note was delivered to The Hague, falsely accusing the Dutch government of having taken the initiative in the conflict by opening their territory to the French and English armies.

There was not enough time to reply to this note; not even enough time to put the agreed defense plan into action: to abandon the north, east, and the major part of the southern parts of the country to hold the Grebbe line (at the frontier of the provinces of Utrecht and Gelderland), then to withdraw progressively behind the old Waterline (flooded line at the frontier of Utrecht, of southern and northern Holland) in order to buy time for the French and English to bring in reinforcements.

The Germans, unfortunately, did not play the game.

They dropped airborne troops behind the Dutch defenses —at Moerdijk, Dordrecht, and Rotterdam—to seize the major bridges and, additionaly, the airfield at The Hague.

Behind the Maas, seizing the bridges here and over the Waal (Dutch Rhine) and over the canal Maas-Waal, Germans—or Dutch Nazis in German uniforms—appeared.

Still, they failed to seize the government, the Queen and the Royal family, in spite of the capture of the airfield and a determined offensive in the center of The Hague. For once, the Dutch were not completely ignorant of the enemy's plans. At six o'clock that first morning, a German transport had crashed right in the center of the Netherlands' capital. In the wreckage the Dutch found a map of the best routes to the center of the city and the royal residence of Scheveningue, plus the following instructions:

"In the combat zone, German civilians are ready to execute the orders they have received. They hold a particular type of permit. The troops owe them total support."

Such a permit was later found on a soldier killed at The Hague:

"Mr. ———— is authorized to cross the German lines to accomplish his mission. The Army must give him maximum assistance at all times. This permit is only valid if it is produced together with an identity card and a photograph."

Imagine the effect of such reports on a nation already convinced that Fifth Column supporters were hiding under every bed, on a people fighting on their own soil for the first time since 1795! Panic!

It was impossible for news of the progress of the war and the multiple betrayals not to become exaggerated. The reports were even more distorted because neither the mails nor telephones were working. The Dutch had to be content with heavily-censored newspaper accounts and radio-telephone bulletins. Details were, therefore, passed by word of mouth.

For Christiaan to be able to say: "I told you so!" at the hour of danger was no consolation. When he heard that the bridges at Maestrict and Arnhem had been seized without a fight by German soldiers wearing Dutch police uniforms, rage shook him. His whole world was collapsing. The country was a collection of idiots and bandits—"an immense middle-class decay"—surrounded by a few elite troops who covered up their flight. The government, the Royal Family—the Queen herself!—abandoned the nation in its darkest hours and went to England. It was true then that "the important people always get out of difficulties." That he had always said as much did not spare Christiaan the disillusioning horror of it.

"The Queen is gone! She embarked at the Hook of Holland on a British torpedo boat," Madame Lindemans said, repeating what her son had already heard. "What is going to happen to us?"

Christiaan shrugged wearily. "Nothing more or less than if she were here. Nobody cares, Mummy, if they all leave, these cowards. They have delivered the country to the Nazis. That they run now is only to be expected."

Henk arrived home at this moment, exhausted, breathing hard because he had run all the way from the port with more—and worse—news.

The Dutch had found a plan showing all the gas stations and garages in the country on the body of a dead German. "The garages," Henk repeated, trembling. "All the garages, Krist! They know them—ours and the others!"

Christiaan put his hand gently on his brother's head, to calm him down, pointing out that it didn't matter now. But the boy shook his head.

"That isn't all! At the port there is a large cargo ship flying the Swedish flag. They are unloading German arms and no one is doing anything to stop them! And seaplanes are landing in the harbor. They put rubber rafts in the water and the Nazis use them to reach the docks! Krist! Do you know what people are doing?"

"They are shaking them by the hand?" Christiaan suggested sarcastically.

"No, not quite!" Henk said. "But they are watching it all completely bewildered, and they are asking each other: 'But who can they be?' "

"I don't want you to go walking in the port alone," his mother put in quickly. "Even if all the stories aren't true, it's too dangerous!"

"Not true?" Henk cried. "But I *saw* them—German soldiers! They have plans of the town and the children of the

Deutsche Schule [German school] are showing them the way when necessary."

It was May 13. There was worse to come. The next day, when Holland did not surrender fast enough, Hermann Goering decided to bomb Rotterdam and threatened to destroy all of Holland's cities if the Dutch did not put down their arms. In Holland, the French and English were carrying on delaying actions to cover up the departure of the Royal Family and government and the Dutch Navy.

The weather was again splendid on May 14 when, during the first hours of the morning, the German High Command asked for—and obtained—the surrender of Rotterdam. But there were still blocks of resistance and Berlin was impatient that the little country had not been brought to its knees in four days. Goering decided to bomb Rotterdam anyway.

The Lindemans were at lunch. It was one-thirty when the first German planes dived down on the center of the city and to the east. Christiaan put down his cup of coffee and listened, his head cocked.

"The Stukkas!" he said after a few seconds.

The German bombers, identifiable by their distinctive, infernal whistling noise, were diving down on their helpless objective. By three-thirty, it was all over.

Christiaan, ignoring his mother's frightened objections, decided to go and look.

What he saw was a horrifying nightmare. The center of the city was in ruins, a blazing inferno. The fire raged long after the enemy planes departed. The rumored number of victims increased hour after hour. They talked of 10,000, 20,000 and then 30,000 people crushed in the smoking ruin of their homes, drowned or burned alive when water and gas tanks exploded.

A dense circle of stupefied spectators surrounded the area, advancing or falling back, depending on the fire's will. For a long time, it was impossible to reach the injured who could be heard moaning or calling for help. They were trapped in a hell of fire and rubble.

In the watching crowd, women cried softly. "Help them!" a girl standing near Christiaan begged. "Help them!"

He shook his head. "We can do nothing for them," he

said. "Even if we could get them out, the hospitals are full already and in a bad way—short of supplies."

Like the others, he was a helpless witness to the martyrdom of his city—fists clinched, face contorted, the rage of the vanquished in his heart.

It was reported that 150,000 had been left homeless by the senseless bombing attack. When Christiaan learned, a few days later while helping to clear away the rubble, that architects, building contractors and municipal magistrates were already at work, poring over plans and a budget for the reconstruction of Rotterdam, agreeing to set certain prices to avoid a future rise in prices, he was filled with contempt.

"They can only think of money," he told his mother. "In a few days we have been flattened, thousands killed and why? Because the government didn't care. They knew they would be able to take shelter. Those who remain, the middle class, think only of themselves. You'll see them increasing the ranks of Mussert's Nazis. It's sickening!"

In vain, his mother tried to calm him down, pointing out that God had spared them—his parents, his brothers, even their friends were safe. But Christiaan refused to be appeased.

In the days that followed, he observed, with ever more disgust, the political game being played in Rotterdam. He listened to people say they were pleased because the German occupation troops behaved "correctly." He despised those who talked of forming a new Dutch government acceptable to Hitler.

"They fight," he told his family, "over who will be Minister, not having fought on the battlefields, but you will see that Hitler will make them agree on who *he* wants!"

He was quite right. On May 29, 1940, at Binnehof, The Hague, in the very room where in the past Queen Wilhelmina had presided over the solemn opening of parliament, Arthur Seyss-Inquart, an Austrian who helped betray his homeland to Hitler in March, 1938, was installed as the Commissioner of the Reich for the Netherlands.

That evening Henk brought home a newspaper which gave the entire text of the ceremony. The entire family read and re-read it. It was ambiguous. They read passages such as these:

"The Germans neither want to oppress the country and population in an imperialistic way, nor impose the German political doctrine. Their activity will be limited by the necessities which arise from the state of war . . . We know that the Führer's final object is peace and order for all men of good will. For Holland shelters 'a brother nation of the German race' and will no doubt gladly take its place in the grandiose reconstruction of 'the new European order.' "

The comments at the Lindemans house were, for the most part, unfavorable. But in the discussion, Christiaan was strangely silent.

He knew one thing already. "The brother nation" did not want to know anything about the "new German order." The Dutch rejected it; they were already preparing themselves to fight, developments which would put Seyss-Inquart on the road to more and more savage repressions.

Not that that bothered him terribly. A dyed-in-the-wool Nazi, when he found he could not make the Dutch "listen to reason," he left the stage clear for the Gestapo, the Abwehr, the SD (*Sicherheitsdienst*—SS intelligence service) and a few other repressive departments.

When, at the end of the war, Seyss-Inquart voluntarily gave himself up to the British, he assured them that "he had only been doing his duty." He heard without wincing the announcement that his name was on the list of Nazi war criminals.

"This type of thing leaves me cold," he told a high-ranking British officer, who answered: "I think, in fact, that is exactly how it will leave you."

But during the spring of 1940, Seyss-Inquart was thinking about effectively ensuring the capitulation of the Netherlands. With him to "help make Holland a province of Great Germany" came four General *Kommissares:* Hanns Albin Rauter (Security and Police) representing Himmler's Gestapo under the title of Hohere und Policier Führer; Friedrich Wimmer (Administration and Justice); Hans Fischbocke (Economy and Finance) and Fritz Schmidt (in charge of "special queries" representing Martin Bormann). The first three men were Austrians; the last—Schmidt—a Westphalian.

For military matters not raised directly by the OKW, they depended on the *"Wehrmachthefehshaben in den Neiger-*

lander" entrusted to General Friedrich Christiansen, an ardent Nazi, who was destined to play the inglorious role of garrison commander.

Of these men the most hated and feared—practically the only one who counted in the eyes of the Dutch—was Rauter, in charge of the police and the SS.

He was a big thin man with brown eyes in a narrow, scarred face. He resembled a Balkan vulture. Born on February 4, 1895, at Klagenfort, in Corinthe, the son of a forest ranger, he volunteered in 1914 for the Austrian mountain troops. He tried his hand in 1918 in the extreme right free corps of Yugoslavia, Poland and Austria.

Christiaan and others learned to call him "Rauter the Executioner." It was Rauter the Executioner who dispelled any illusions about the possibilities of coexistence between the conquerors and the conquered.

As the Germans moved in, the Lindemans—for once all of the same opinion—had only sickening contempt for those Dutchmen who turned the administrative, financial and economic machinery of the country over to the Germans. The Lindemans jeered at the Council of Secretaries General who called themselves Ministers.

Badly prepared for the part they had to play, these Dutch were, on the one hand, proud of getting a hand in "running the country" (an illusion the German's didn't indulge them in for long) and had, on the other, trouble ignoring the barbarous side of Nazi methods. Along with many of their countrymen, these Dutch civil servants found themselves on the horns of a dilemma.

Should one collaborate, they asked themselves, or resist? Should one turn the economic machinery to the greatest interest of the conqueror? Or should one stop it or use it against the enemy—which would leave the Dutch without work and end in having more of them sent to Germany to do forced labor? Should one stay at one's post to avoid having the government of the country fall into the hands of Mussert's Dutch Nazis? Or should one quit and let the Germans muddle through?

Belgium and France capitulated in June 1940. England's future would no doubt be decided in a few weeks. These

Dutch told themselves to accept the inevitable—which meant a long period of German supremacy.

In this confusion, the Dutch political parties were silent. The left wing decided to claim the Resistance, hoping to turn the center and right wing away from collaboration— while their numbers were still few—and push the enemy out. The Dutch people were delighted with the spontaneous demonstration of June 29, 1940, when everyone came out of his home wearing a white carnation—the favorite flower of Prince Bernhard whose birthday it was.

Now the Lindemans were quarreling again. All of them were putting their hopes in the House of Orange as the symbol of liberty. All of them, that is, except Christiaan. He joked bitterly about the stupidity of putting one's trust in people who abandoned them when they were needed most.

His parents answered that it was better for the country to have the Dutch Royal Family and government in exile than as prisoners or puppets of the Nazis, like King Leopold of Belgium.

Christiaan could not agree. He began to spend more and more of his time doing nothing, loitering at the cafes, drinking too much and picking up prostitutes. He refused to work in the family garage—not that there was that much to do— and despised his older brother who had quietly picked up his work again.

The arguments between them grew more and more frequent and more and more serious. And Henk listened, wide-eyed, always on Christiaan's side.

The boy agreed, for instance, when Christiaan pointed out that where Dutch industry was being maintained, it was fulfilling German orders; that food produced on Dutch farms took the road to the Third Reich.

The eldest Lindemans son retorted: "You are so cocksure —you know everything. But the authorities are also stock-piling food for the future!"

"Stocks that the Germans know about and will seize when they need them," Krist countered.

"What do you know about it?" his brother challenged. "As for the factories, if they shut down, the workers will be sent to Germany."

"They aren't shutting down!" shouted Christiaan. "In fact,

the shareholders are growing rich. But this still doesn't stop trainloads of workers from leaving for Germany every day. And what happens if they manage to escape and get back? Their fellow workers and employers are so scared of reprisals, they advise them to return to Germany!" In fact, by the end of that year—1940—140,000 Dutch were forced to leave their homeland for factories inside Germany.

"Those who think like that are a minority," Christiaan's brother answered patiently.

"Perhaps, but that is still too many," Krist said. "Haven't you noticed how difficult it is for the poor, how sick they look, that their clothes hang on their thin bodies? They will be cold this winter!"

"It is the common destiny," his brother said pompously.

At that, Christiaan really blew up. "Is that true, bureaucrat? Those who have country homes are stockpiling food. The rich construct bunkers and mysterious launching platforms and do not lack for anything. In the big hotels, everything goes on as before. Rationing doesn't exist for them. . . ."

The argument was like a dialogue between the deaf which could go on forever. Still, in the end, the Lindemans all joined the Resistance—each doing what he could, each for his own reasons. But Christiaan was the only one to give himself totally to the fight against the Occupation.

During the first year of the war, he was discontented, at loose ends, criticizing everything, trying to find a quick answer to why the Dutch had reacted so badly.

Now he embarked on the road to danger, joy, devotion, deception, loyalty—and, ultimately, betrayal. As the Resistance fighters moved along the road they chose, they repeated to themselves: "Live like the fish of the depths—agitate and do the rounds, but do it quietly."

This was how they came to be known as "those who plunge into the depths" (to disappear from the official administrative community). The *"onderduikers"*—divers. Under cover, the Dutch Resistance organized itself, carefully serving its apprenticeship.

There were many reasons why Christiaan made his decision. Patriotism, fired by Nazi oppression. Shame at the cowardice of some of his countrymen. A hunger for adventure; the need to experience danger and violence. The need for revenge. The need for acceptance . . . admiration. His motives were complicated and he could not express them.

Whatever they were, he was destined to face many dangers on the road ahead as he moved, all unknowing, toward his tragic destiny.

CHAPTER FIVE

Queen Wilhelmina had not intended to run away; she had only wanted to reach Flessingue. However, she had not reckoned with the commander of the British torpedo boat who had taken her on board.

He did not want to risk being taken prisoner, along with his vessel and crew. In addition, he had received orders from the Admiralty to take the Dutch Queen to London. King Haakon of Norway was already there.

As a result, the entire Dutch Executive found itself in England, joining the Ministers who had fled earlier.

Churchill, in his memoirs, relates the scene on the evening of May 10, 1940, when he returned from the Admiralty after making preparations for his accession to the post of Prime Minister, replacing Neville Chamberlain:

"The Dutch Ministers, were waiting for me. Haggard, exhausted, their eyes full of horror, they had just arrived from Amsterdam. Their country had been attacked without the slightest warning, the slightest pretext.

"An avalanche of flames and steel had broken loose on the frontiers and when the Dutch had opened fire, the Germans retaliated with violent air attacks. The whole country was the prey of confusion. . . . The Ministers asked for help. The Queen was still in the Netherlands but it did not seem as though she would stay there very long. . . . Even after the recent invasion of Norway and Denmark, the Dutch Ministers did not seem to understand that Germany—who until the day before had been friendly—could have launched itself into this dreadfully brutal operation."

And the man who was going to lead England in war added later:

"Mr. Colijn—then Prime Minister, when he had come to see me in 1937—had exposed the marvelous effectiveness of the possibilities of flooding. He could, he said, while sitting at my table at Chartwell, push a button via a phone call, thus drawing up an impassable barrier of water.

"But all of this had vanished like a dream, showing that in our era a little country cannot oppose alone the greed of a great nation.

"Everywhere the Germans had passed they had taken possession of the bridges and canals, the locks and points of water distribution. In only one day, they had captured the advanced defences of Holland. At the same time, their aviation crushed the defenseless country. Rotterdam was on fire, a ruin. The same fate threatened The Hague, Utrecht, and Amsterdam. The hope that the Dutch had nourished—to see the German army pass on their right and save themselves— was in vain. Nevertheless, under the blow the whole nation rose with indomitable courage. Queen Wilhelmina, her family, the members of her government, reached Great Britain, thanks to the Royal Navy. They continued to serve as inspiration to their people, to administer their vast empire across the seas. The Dutch Navy and the considerable merchant fleet of this country were placed without reservation under British control, playing a formidable part in the allied battle. . . . I asked the War Office to draw up plans for the use of a Dutch Brigade, as the government in exile desired. . . ."

Naturally, things did not go at all as planned. The Queen, her family and the government in exile were far from serving as an inspiration to the people, who were completely cut off from the rest of the world and shocked by the precipitate departure of the nation's whole Executive.

That nearly all the Dutch war fleet—3,100 sailors—all the merchant fleet and 1,500 officers, soldiers and policemen had reached England to continue the fight from there did give the Dutch people hope. But towards the leaders of their country, their attitude was much cooler.

In addition, throughout the war there was tension and a certain amount of misunderstanding between the Resistance in Great Britain and the Resistance in Holland. Depending on the area and the individuals, the breach was more or less severe. As far as Christiaan Lindemans was concerned, there were "good people" in London who fought according to the traditional rules, played the secret war with more or less success (rather less than more), whereas in the Netherlands they were trapped by the tragic reality of the occupation. The Resistance had not yet formed a select club; it was still busy weeding out the weak, the indecisive, the timid and the over-scrupulous.

This probably explains the distressing failure of the first Dutch secret mission to the Netherlands. It was set up by the prefect of police at The Hague, F. van t'Sant, who had become secretary to the Queen. He had managed to put the beginnings of a Dutch secret service in exile on its feet, the *Centrale Inlichtingendienst*. On August 28, 1940, in agreement with the English, it parachuted a young marine officer, Lado van Hamel, "blind" near Leyde. ("Blind": no advance notice.)

For six weeks, he tried without success to establish radio contact with London and to form Resistance groups. He mainly approached the military, putting the first elements of the *Orde Dienst* on its feet. He was not overly successful. England was so unaware of the conditions of life in an occupied country that they had neglected to furnish Van Hamel with the means to perform the normal activities of an agent on a mission. It was not surprising that the Germans immediately put him under surveillance, and that they had no difficulty in stopping him as soon as they realized he was about to go back and report to his superiors. Lado van Hamel was shot in June, 1941.

This failure, combined with the failures of two missions that arrived in the Netherlands by seaplane during the sum-

mer of 1940, caused the exiled Dutch to review their infiltra-
tion methods. They replaced Van t'Sant's service with two
others: the BVT (Return Preparations Office) and the MUT
(Military Return Preparations Office).

On July 28, 1940, Queen Wilhelmina inaugurated "Radio
Orange"; she did not even know if anyone was listening, or,
indeed, even if she could be heard. Occupied Holland did
not realize it but the Cavalier of Geer, shattered by the defeat, pessimistic, faint-hearted, and crushed by the unfolding
of the battle of England, was pleading with the Queen and
his fellow Ministers to negotiate with Hitler for a separate
peace! He was later replaced by Doctor Pieter S. Gerbrandy.

It is certain that if the Dutch had been able to follow the
day-by-day existence of their government in exile, they would
have lost what little respect they had left for it. As Louis de
Jong wrote: "Everybody blames the political parties for the
blindness shown . . ."

Dark rivalry and hypocrisy, which were not admitted at
the time, existed between the Resistance at home and the
exiled government. Later, after the war, they blamed each
other for various mistakes.

This rivalry was partly a result of the ignorance of the
men who were isolated so long in Great Britain, losing touch
with the real political and material situation on the Continent.
It was also one of the reasons for the terrible slaughter of
agents in the secret services. If the officers who followed the
Queen into exile had not thought of leaving behind them the
nucleus of an intelligence organization, the British had done
no better.

According to the custom of the secret services, the English
had before the war covered the sensitive zones of Europe
with well-trained "information" systems. *"La Service Continental"* (Continental Service) was set up near "sensitive countries," for example, up to mid-August 1938, in Vienna, with
the British Passport Office as cover. Thomas Kendrick was
in charge. When, in March, 1938, Hitler annexed Austria,
Kendrick promptly burnt all his records. This led to the
customary exchange of notes and other diplomatic niceties
and ended, on August 22, 1938, with Kendrick being sent
back to his native country.

The Continental Service was next installed in Copenhagen

until, in November, 1938, the Danes decided to cleanse their country of a number of spies they believed to be working for Hitler's Germany. Thus they stopped a certain Waldeman Poetzsch—much to the satisfaction of the Abwehr, who knew him to be an English agent. When they realized their mistake, the Danes were very apologetic, but it was too late and the service had to be moved again, this time to The Hague.

Just before the war the organization was reformed, branched out and divided into sections (political, economic, military, maritime, counter-espionage), under the leadership of Major Henry Richard Stevens. Among the officers placed under his command, as the head of the military section, was Captain Payton Sigmund Best, a resident in Holland since the First World War.

In 1939, Reinhard Heydrich, boss of the S.D., *Sicherheitsdienst,* intelligence department of the Nazi S.S., took offense over this section which was becoming too active. He infiltrated an agent who pretended he was in contact with a certain "Major Solms" of the Luftwaffe, fundamentally anti-Nazi. Solms seemed to be the center of a plot against Hitler, stirred up by him and by a group of friends. A plot which—if the English gave them a hand, the agent hinted—had a wonderful chance of success.

Of course, Solms would only agree to talk to high-ranking officers, whom he offered to meet in a little village near the German frontier called Venlo. He explained that he dared not meet them on Dutch soil for fear of drawing too much attention in Berlin to his movements.

Captain Best met Solms at Venlo. Solms was a gigantic Bavarian, confident, quick-tempered, who boasted loudly, but nevertheless, was only a messenger. During the second meeting, Solms made an "accidental" allusion to "a general" who hoped to open up talks with the English. In view of the importance of these new developments, Best judged he should tell his superior, Major Stevens, and take his orders for a third rendezvous, which took place in Duixpenlo (a Dutch village on the frontier).

This seemed so promising that another meeting was arranged at Venlo, for November 9, 1939. The British agents were, in fact, at last going to meet the famous "General" and learn from him what he expected from them.

The meeting was arranged for 1600 hours, in a little red-brick café, the Bachus, an isolated shack in a lonely area less than 200 metres from the German border. When the English arrived, the frontier barrier was lifted on the German side. On the terrace of the Bachus, a familiar silhouette—Solms—gestured to them. Suddenly, a large fast car came into view from the direction of Germany. It was filled with armed soldiers who quickly surrounded the two agents, captured them and took them across the frontier without further ado. The detachment in charge of this mission was commanded by a young twenty-eight-year-old German officer who was going to be much talked about: Walter Schellenberg. The operation properly decapitated the English service center at 15 Nieuwe Uitweg in The Hague. It was completely crossed off the intelligence map in May, 1940, when an agent fled forgetting to take a suitcase with him in which the Germans found—among other things—a list of British spies complete with addresses and code names.

Nobody was more grieved about this chain of events than the Abwehr. German Military Intelligence had been keeping an eye on the officers in The Hague for some time. From time to time, a canalboat would moor almost in front of the offices. Through a porthole, the Germans filmed the comings and goings at 15 Nieuwe Uitweg, and they had the names, false names, covers, and activities to go with the faces.

If S. D. chief Heydrich and Abwehr chief Admiral Wilhelm Canaris had not hated each other so, they would probably have agreed to let the "Continental Service" stay in business and "poison it" within the usual traditions of the game, which would certainly have been more profitable. When a service is destroyed it's replaced with a new network and it takes time and effort to identify the new agents. However, the Wehrmacht redeemed Heydrich's error. The fall of Belgium and of France, the occupation of Western Europe in July, 1940, completely cut off the English from the Continent.

In order to reconstitute the network, they would have to work under new conditions, up till then unknown to the classic secret services. Something original would have to be arranged—to fight a subversive war. To the necessity of inventing, bit by bit, unorthodox forms of secret war, were added the exceptionally difficult working conditions.

The services depending on the army also had to reconstitute their networks. They infiltrated their own agents, installed offices at Berne, Lisbon, Madrid, Gibraltar and Stockholm. They had their own sources of information, their own escape routes, and their own transmitters.

But it was still necessary, however, to create a new system, in charge of co-ordination, to investigate the possibilities of "subversive action and sabotage, and gather information in occupied countries."

On July 1, 1940, Churchill okayed the establishment of such a system. On the 16th, he chose a Labour Minister, Hugh Dalton, to lead it. On the 19th, the service received its title, and on the 22nd it was approved by the War Cabinet. So the SOE—Special Operations Executive—which the English modestly called the "service of ungentlemanly warfare," was born. It inspired the Americans to create their OSS (Office of Strategic Services).

The SOE consisted of a number of general branches (liaison, finances, transmissions, supplies, etc.), plus three or four large geographic branch groupings. The most important, the Northern European Branch, a "London Group," was also in charge of preparing agents in a series of specialized schools or sections. "Section N" or the "Dutch Section," was commanded by an Englishman—at first, Major Seymour Bingham—in liaison with a Dutch officer, Colonel de Bruyene.

The SOE had to surmount a lot of opposition and unfavourable prejudice, internal and external. At first, the military saw it in a very bad light. Michael Foot said of the SOE in France: "There was a certain aversion among the regular officers to the Resistance. They saw it as an irresponsible military organization, too left wing. . . ."

But England was not on the verge of landing in force on the Continent. She urgently needed to find eyes and ears for the day when she could begin the offensive. During the interval, she had to content herself with tormenting Germany, with keeping the enemy off-balance, with rendering the occupation as difficult as possible. In every possible way, the enemy had to be deprived through sabotage and other means of the essential materials he needed to run his war machine.

As David Galula said "in the fight between the lion and the fly, the fly does not possess the same strength as the lion, but the lion cannot steal so easily."

The SOE, in this light, became the instrument of a sort of revolutionary war. However, neither England nor the governments in exile wanted it to go too far. It was intended to create, encourage, help, and direct a revolt against the enemy and against the Nazi system—not to encourage the total reform of society as it was before the war. The constant friction between the SOE and the Resistance movements was the result of the vast variety of political opinions to be found in them and the split between those who had their minds on the present and those who had their eyes on the future.

In addition, there were strong conflicts between the SOE and the refugee governments in London. The English insisted that all the agents should be briefed in their centers and surrounded in the field by the SOE officers. All messages concerning them had to pass via the British transmission centers, the personnel of which came either from the Royal Corps of Signals or from the FANYs.

Where the Dutch were concerned, for example, radio-transmitters, the codes, the telegraph keys, were furnished and known only by the English. They alone saw the messages on arrival or departure in their entirety.

The Germans knew all about this conflict and used it as fuel for their anti-English propaganda. But the Resistance obstinately refused to allow any of this to affect its operations.

The German propaganda only became active in 1942. Up till then, the Nazis did not believe that a widespread English underground action existed, preferring to believe that they were simply dealing with the spontaneous efforts of local groups promoting raids, sabotage, propaganda and general disruption. It was partly true. The British penetration into the Low Countries had been very weak before 1942; the efforts of the SOE were hardly felt, compared to the actions of the national movements.

If Resistance groups like the Legion of Front Line Soldiers or the Orange Guard were squashed almost immediately; if the leaders of the *Orde Dienst* or *Les Gueux* were quickly located, identified, unmasked, and executed, other men still remained and fresh networks appeared in their places.

Clandestine newspapers, bases of movements such as *Les Gueux, Je maintiendrai, Vrij Nederland, De Vrij Katheder, Het Parool, Trouw*, etc., lived, in fact, by their own means, carrying out their own fight.

Added to this was the action of public protests, such as strikes.

The strikes formed one of the most outstanding aspects of the Dutch Resistance. There were three. Two of them were created by the general opposition to the Nazi's anti-Jewish measures. The third erupted at the time of Arnhem, and its object was to paralyze the life of the Low Countries and hamper the resistance of the German troops.

The first strike in the Low Countries was that of the students at Leyde and at Delft, who in autumn, 1940, were deprived of their Jewish lecture.

The second took place in February, 1941. At that time, Mussert's Nazis were urged by the German masters to spread out through the Jewish district of Amsterdam, ransacking the shops, breaking everything in their path, and stirring up real riots.

"This bestiality, a few feet away from the venerable Synagogue and from the house where Rembrandt had lived and painted, prompted horror and indignation," Louis de Jong wrote.

Finally, on February 22 and 23, under the eye of an already sensitive population, the first round-up of the Jews took place. They did not believe that they would be sent to their death at Manthausen, but they knew enough to feel sick.

Holland had never heard of the "Jewish Question." Out of 140,000 Jews, 70,000 lived in Amsterdam. These Jews were old Dutch families who had lived in Holland for centuries (with the exception of political refugees from Germany or Austria since Hitlerism). The Dutch, when asked, haughtily said that they knew no Jews, only compatriots or friends.

When the Jews were excluded from public employment, the other Dutch officials told Seyss-Inquart that this did not help their task. When they were forbidden to use public transport, public libraries, to go to the theatre or to the cinema; when Jewish enterprises were obliged to declare themselves (so the businesses could be confiscated); when Jewish doctors were allowed only to nurse Jews, thousands of Dutchmen answered back by patronizing Jewish shops and lining up outside the doors of Jewish doctors.

It was "this bad spirit" that Seyss-Inquart and Rauter wanted to destroy—and the country answered with a general strike. Everything stopped: tramways, electricity, gas, sanitary services, factories, deliveries of agricultural produce, naval channel and port traffic. The reprisals were terrible. Hostages were taken and shot. Thousands went into hiding, joining the ranks of the *onderduikers*.

Collective fines were forced from the towns: £1,500,000 for Amsterdam, £250,000 for Hilversum, and £50,000 for Zaandam. The municipal Dutch Counsels were dissolved and replaced by commissioners from the Gestapo. The state of siege, proclaimed in February, lasted a good month. For the first time, the Germans came up against a determined, organized opposition from the population and they realized that if the English were able to arm and command this opposition, the situation in the Netherlands would rapidly become intolerable.

It was then that Gestapo Chief Himmler decided to send a few specialists in subversive war to the Netherlands.

Until the strikes of 1941, the Gestapo and the SD had been weakly represented in Holland. The Abwehr, too, had only one relatively quiet office, headed by Colonel Hofwald, a stout and fearful man who disliked trouble. He was perfectly satisfied to leave the coast clear to the leader of the Amt IV of the Sicherheitsdienst, who landed in October 1940 and who, up to 1941, managed its duties.

But at the beginning of 1941, two new men arrived: Kriminalrat Schreieder for the Gestapo and, for the Abwehr, Colonel Hermann Giskes, transferred from the Lutetia Hotel in Paris to The Hague.

Giskes took up his post—without satisfaction and during a torrential rain—troubled by the welcome which awaited him. In France, he told himself, at least one knew where one stood. One fought in enemy country. But here, everything was very different.

Giskes had wonderful memories of the few days he had spent in The Hague two years before, but things had changed considerably. While driving along roads lacquered with rain,

e asked himself why the Dutch counter-espionage effort
was being strengthened suddenly.

Colonel Hofwald received him . . . without reassurance.
An officer of the old school, a bit hard of hearing, he was
above all a diplomat.

He showed Giskes Schevenigue House, a large square
structure of white stone with a view of the North Sea and
a shore that day deserted, icy, surrendering to the bombard-
ment of the waves whose foaming crests seemed to reflect
the heavy clouds which hurried across the sky.

The mess was close by, situated in another villa, small,
solidly built and comfortable. The officers of the III F
section, however, occupied Hooweg, a handsome home built
in 19th Century style. A high steel gate and fence encircled a
garden, separating it from the seldom used road which was
planted with lime trees. On the other side of this road there
were no houses, but open fields and then woods. It was easy
to watch the road from the house, yet difficult to watch the
house from the road. A concealed door led to the HQ's
mess. A tunnel communicated directly with the center of the
town, emerging not far from Binnenhof. The only close
neighbor to his retreat (that Giskes baptized immediately
"The Citadel") was the naval commander-in-chief of the
Netherlands. Nothing could have been more discreet.

The personnel, however, left much to be desired. Giskes
rapidly asked for the authority to sack most of them and
replace them with men of his own choice. In the end, he
kept only two people from the old establishment: a Captain
Wurr and an interpreter named Willy Kup.

Wurr had been in the infantry during the First World
War. He was no longer a young man, greying, rheumatic,
bad tempered, but with shrewd judgment. He had a suave
accent, liked the easy and comfortable life, but, nevertheless,
retained an alert mind and a keen intelligence.

Questioned by Hermann Giskes, he reported the rumors
about secret arrivals by sea or by air, radio communications
with London, couriers going regularly to Berne, Madrid, or
Stockholm. No coherent organization had yet been precisely
identified. A British seaplane had come several times. Unfortunately, through bad co-ordination between the services,
it was shot down by the Luftwaffe just at the moment when

Intelligence had started to observe it. In Spain, a relay ha
been discovered through which information gathered i
Holland was passed to England. The personal messages c
Radio Orange seemed to prove that secret comings and goin
between the Netherlands and Great Britain were taking plac

Hermann Giskes concluded from all this that a Dutc
Resistance did exist, was in contact with London and vu
nerable, like all secret services, especially at the liaison leve
The first thing, then, would be to reinforce the radio lister
ing posts and locate the radios used by the Resistance.

However, here a difficulty arose. Herr Kriminalra
Schreieder, Sturmbannfuhrer SS, was following the sam
trail with the same methods—but with different objective
Whereas the Abwehr "returned" a large number of agent
Schreieder was a policeman, a man of action, he looked fo
numerous arrests, his goal was repression.

Giskes decided to visit him at Binnenhof and convince hir
that an alliance with the Abwehr would not impede his activ
ities. In fact, it would be beneficial for everybody.

It was a very delicate task, for Schreieder, in spite of
solemn politeness marked by frequent little bows, was
suspicious man. Finally, however, he was convinced, an
from then on the two men formed a dangerous team agains
the resistants.

First, they attacked the *"Orde Dienst"*, a para-militar
organization whose officers were trying to form an informa
tion-gathering service and a secret army at the same time
Their security left a lot to be desired.

Next, Giskes and company attacked the clandestine news
paper groups, the importance of which was often under
estimated. The success of anti-German operations was greatl
affected by those groups. It was thanks to them that th
onderduikers benefited from the protection of a populatio
more and more on the alert, better and better informed. I
was imperative that Holland be prepared for undercove
action. She was a small, overpopulated (at that time ther
were nine million inhabitants) country with a very comple
economy, a very dense and very varied communications ne
work (few areas are more than an hour's walk from a goo
road). There are no mountains, the woods only cover

percent of the territory. All the west of the country is above sea level, the east is easy to penetrate.

One could hardly imagine a nation less well endowed for clandestine pursuits. There was no common frontier with an allied or neutral country. The North Sea was actively patrolled; the Dutch coasts closely watched. The maritime routes were used once in a while by agents, but they always presented great difficulties, whether on the Swedish route (which they had to provisionally abandon several times) or the English route. The air route was no better. Landings or pick-ups—even by the little Lysander—were rendered impossible by the multitude of canals, the difficulty of covering up the operation in a perfectly flat country, and low-lying mists which prevented the plane from seeing the ground lights.

The large transport planes or the seaplanes were up against a gigantic air defense network which stretched out along the road of the industrial reservoir of the Ruhr. The losses were so heavy that these aircraft preferred to drop the men or the material in Belgium.

Christiaan Lindemans was often in charge of retrieving agents or war material and taking them to the Netherlands. He acquired a great reputation as a ferryman and guide with MI-9—the evasion organization of the British Intelligence Service—and in a number of networks such as the CSVI (sabotage and information group directed from London), *Het Parool, Trouw,* the *Resistance Counsel* and Belgian or French Resistance groups that occasionally needed him. There was ample opportunity for him to become a legendary figure.

He had plenty of time, during the years of resistance, to build up this image. He served as ferryman to the most menaced of the *onderduikers* from the early days of the movement. He was one of the first to use the Swedish route (by cargo boats connecting the two countries), going as far as Stockholm himself when necessary.

Smuggling for his own pocket—he specialized for quite a while in cigarette papers—he preferred the Spanish route through Belgium and France, which offered him more money-making possibilities.

During the first days of the Resistance, the networks had not thought of forming real escape channels, independent from the other activities of the movements. They nearly all needed the services of individual ferrymen, and Christiaan was one of them.

He also made contact with the first registered resistance movement: *Les Gueux*. Its members made their first clandestine journey on May 15, 1940, the second a few days later, on May 18. In October, 1940, their organization covered the whole country.

This did not last, for the Gestapo made grave inroads in the movement. Only the newspaper managed to carry on its publication throughout the whole war, though it never reached the circulation of many other organs of the clandestine press, as one can see on the following chart:

Title	Politics	Maximum Circulation
Je maintiendrai	Socialist	50,000
Christoofar	Left-wing Catholic	12,000
De Vonk	Socialist revolutionary	20,000
Vrij Nederland	Socialist independent protestant	80,000
De Vrij Kathedere	Communist, students and artists	5,000
Les Gueux	Students and universities	5,000
Het Parool	Independent socialist	60,000
Trouw	Protestant conservative	130,000
De Waaheid	Communist	50,000

All the clandestine newspapers maintained the fighting spirit of the Dutch and this played an important part in the secret war. Next to the news, they contained articles dedicated to the future of the country and appeals for aid for the *onderduikers*.

The nine papers in the chart were already functioning in 1941. Later the following papers were formed: the *Landelijke Organisatie tot hulp aan Onderduiken* (1942), the *Abeille diligente* (1942), and the *Aussen Minsterris* (1942)—assisted by the organizations of the spiritual Resistance of the Churches, by the National Council, by the Council of the Nine, and by the Medical Contact.

The active military or political resistance organizations through necessity changed a lot over the war years, constantly altering their make-up according to the repression, executions and escapes that affected them. Thus the following organizations were formed: *Orde Dienst* (military and conservative, the activities of which we have already mentioned); the *Knokploegen* (commandos specializing in raids on civilian or supply offices); the *Raad van Verzet,* or RVV (left-wing organization which often used Christiaan Lindemans' services not only as a guide but also as a member of military expeditions); and the *Pilotess Hulp* ("aid to the pilots") which combined a number of escape networks and got its name from the fact that several of its systems got started by aiding shot-down allied pilots and returning them to Great Britain.

The "political resistance" was the last to really get organized. These groups include: *La Grande Commission Consultaire de L'illegalite,* the *Commission de Contact,* and the *College des Hommes de Confiance.* Their members were subject to strict rules, but little attention was given to the most important commodity: secrecy.

For this type of Resistance organization, Christiaan had only contempt. He made war; such groups only carried on sterile debates. If *Trouw* and *Het Parool* escaped his reprobation, it was because—besides their newspapers—they had "active" resistance networks which often called on him.

So we find him, during the war years, mixed up in the adventures of a number of secret groups, because the Resistance in Holland—as elsewhere, or perhaps more so than elsewhere—was divided, changeable, mobile (in such a way that it is impossible today to draw up a complete list of networks). It easily used the same men in a variety of jobs in different systems.

Christiaan Lindemans was the perfect illustration of this. He served as ferryman, courier, liaison agent, saboteur, information agent, network leader. He loved the challenge and the danger. He loved to hear people say that only he could carry out such-and-such a task well. He never refused a mission—whatever the risk.

He was the perfect choice when the Anglo-Dutch forces decided to infiltrate a "double agent" into the German services, which were raising hell with the underground in Holland.

CHAPTER SIX

Life was increasingly difficult in occupied Holland, in 1941. The rationing, rising prices, restrictions on traveling, the curfew and the rioting got worse as each day passed.

The war dragged on. After the euphoria of the RAF victory in the "Battle of Britain" and the hope raised by the Soviet Union's entry into the war, Holland fell back into despair, as weeks and months passed without any foreseeable end to the fighting.

Without work, for naturally the family business had suffered badly, Christiaan killed time wandering from cafe to cafe and chasing after the girls. He camouflaged his Resistance activities by trafficking in contraband—which had the double advantage of filling his wallet and furnishing him with an alibi for his journeys. They said of him later that he had a kind heart and never refused help to those who needed it.

Perhaps his generosity was partly to blame for his eventual downfall. More likely it was his connection with a group of people who were only out to make money from the war.

He formed what turned out to be a fatal relationship with three men at this time: George Ridderhof, Albert Brinkman and Henk Jandoel, with whom, at first glance, he seemed to have nothing in common.

George Ridderhof looked like a tramp. Weak, shabby, unclean, he had recently been released from prison. He boasted about his dealings with drug traffickers and jewel thieves and claimed to be a contraband specialist. Christiaan took his stories with a very large pinch of salt. The man, he thought, was in no shape for such an active, dangerous life. He was fat, bloated from too much alcohol, and had a bad left leg. When he was drunk—which was often—he spoke a mixture of English, Spanish, and Dutch learned in the slums of Indonesia.

Christiaan would never have tolerated him if he hadn't been a friend of Henk Jandoel. Jandoel was known as an "honorable" merchant with a shop of his own where he sold surgical instruments. He was a big, robust, always cheerful man with a clear, round face who looked younger than the thirty-five years he claimed. He spoke German and French as well as Dutch.

The third man, Albert Brinkman, was a friend of Christiaan's from the Resistance whom he introduced to the other two. Brinkman (also known as Bingham and sometimes Van Straaten) belonged to a CSVI group and used a network of SOE radio operators recruited mainly from among Dutch students for his contacts with London.

But Brinkman's principal attraction for Christiaan was that he had a very beautiful woman, Lydia Fick, set up in a charming flat in the Plaats, in The Hague, and he traveled frequently. While he was gone, Christiaan often visited Lydia, to keep her from getting bored. Christiaan and Brinkman each led a rather active love life. Neither took the other seriously and they got on well together.

Later, two other men joined this "select" group: Cornelius Verloop and Anthony Damen. The pair was to have a disastrous influence on Christiaan's destiny.

The group's common bond was pleasure; they were out strictly to have a good time. Their escapades were usually financed by Jandoel, whose business seemed to be more and more prosperous; by Brinkman, who seemed to have unlimited funds and, sometimes, by Ridderhof. Christiaan was more often broke than not, but he contributed generously to the communal diversions when he had the means.

The company of these men encouraged Christiaan to accentuate ever more the cynical, anarchist side of his nature, so much so that a number of his friends in the networks had trouble recognizing in him sometimes the troubled, impulsive, but courageous and sincere young man they had first known.

He was traveling a lot these days. He accomplished a number of escort missions for different resistance groups—in particular for a small network connected with the Dutch-Paris group and directed from Paris by a Doctor de Voss. This encouraged him to set up his own relay system—in Holland, Belgium, France, right up to the Spanish border. He decided to set up a central base of operations in Lille.

He needed a discreet and safe refuge. Naturally, it was a woman, Gilou Lelup, who provided it. A cabaret singer, she was to bear him a lovely blonde daughter whom Christiaan adored. Gilou offered him not only the shelter of her home and her arms, but her courage. More than once she undertook missions for him. Thanks to Gilou, his life regained a certain stability and for a time—until 1943—he was less directly influenced by his questionable playmates. Gilou understood him and reassured him, and his life in the Resistance satisfied his need for power and recognition. He was admired all over the networks for his exploits; he was important—someone to look up to.

His double life—as a cynical, devil-may-care contrabandist and a daring Resistance agent—called for constant subterfuge.

To cover up a sudden departure from Rotterdam on Resistance business, he would tell Jandoel: "Henk, old man, I must go to Paris. I have been given the address of a fantastic club where the champagne is first class and the girls—like that!"

Jandoel would laugh and wink and nod his head knowingly. Neither he nor Ridderhof ever suspected their friend Krist's undercover activities, which was fortunate because Ridderhof was a paid agent of the Abwehr and a clever one. Christiaan, who disliked Ridderhof from the beginning, was puzzled by Henk Jandoel's friendship with him. Henk was such a simple, frank, open fellow.

For instance, it was hard to resist Jandoel when he begged him, as he was about to leave on one of his journeys: "Krist, I would like to come with you to Paris (or Lille or Brussels)." And Christiaan, after first trying to dissuade him, would usually agree, planning to shake him at the earliest opportunity. He liked his company and besides Jandoel always had plenty of money with him. And he knew he would have no trouble shaking him when it was time to carry out his mission. All he had to say was that he had a date with some girl (which was sometimes true) and Jandoel would laugh and say, "How do you do it? What do the women see in you?"

And Christiaan would leave him, still laughing and shaking his head.

Jandoel would wander around on his own then, taking in the sights of the town, or sometimes he would look up a friend to spend an hour or so with. Paul, for example.

Paul, like Ridderhof, was not in the least attractive. Tall, thin, redheaded, with a mangy moustache, a shifty expression and too-small eyes which were too close together, he inspired no sympathy. He talked endlessly—too much, Jandoel often said to himself, for he really got very bored.

Paul also traveled a lot, disappearing for days and weeks without saying why. But when he was at Lille at the same time as Jandoel, the two were inseparable. Christiaan, who'd met Paul, couldn't understand it. Things would have been clearer if he had known that Paul ran an escape network for "Pat O'Leary" and that he had been "returned" by the Germans—in fact, by Henk Jandoel.

Who, then, was this man Christiaan knew as Henk Jandoel and who one member of *Orde Dienst* thought he recognized as a Frenchman named Hermann Eberte, an old agent of the *Duxieme Bureau?*

At the registry office, he was listed as Richard-Louis-Guillaume Christmann, born at Metz in 1905. But he often used his mother's maiden name—in either the French or the German form—and called himself "Arnaud" or "Arno." He had become the "friend" of Herman Giskes, in so far as he was capable of friendship, in spite of their differences in rank, origin and mentality. As well as he could, Giskes always protected this agent.

Christmann, alias Jandoel, had had an eventful youth, volunteering for the Foreign Legion which he left to enter the services of the French *Deuxieme Bureau.* Badly paid—at least he thought so—he let himself be used by the Germans in 1937. His ability to speak both French and German was an asset both sides appreciated.

In 1940, he surfaced in Paris after the surrender, wearing the uniform of a *"Sander führer,"* which he rapidly abandoned for a well-cut civilian suit to join the Abwehr under Colonel Friederich Rudolph. He did his job well, penetrating the French Resistance under various names. He found his German masters were very resourceful people. He was allowed to participate in "the transfer of Jewish possessions" and keep a generous slice for himself. His relations with contraband and drug traffic units kept his wallet full.

Hermann Giskes greatly appreciated his talents. He even seemed to believe—and yet Giskes was not naive—in his sincerity and "patriotism."

In fact, Christmann/Jandoel had no allegiance to any country. Without roots and with no desire to put any down, he was prepared to serve the highest bidder—and the highest bidder at that time was the Abwehr. He became, therefore, "my dear Arno" for Hermann Giskes and frequently visited him after he took up his post at The Hague.

Colonel Giskes was reserving him for a particularly delicate task, giving as the reason the ease with which he could pass for either a Frenchman or a Dutchman. Not only did he want him to penetrate the Resistance escape networks and subvert them, but he wanted him to set up false escape channels (in the beginning, helping real prisoners escape in order to get the reputation for being reliable) to get Abwehr agents into Great Britain, which the German secret services were having the greatest difficulty penetrating.

Another problem for the Abwehr was Dutch radio communication with England. Giskes dreamed of capturing several underground radio-transmitting stations and using them to supply London with false information. This was a delicate operation. To succeed, the Germans would have to know the codes, routines, hours and frequencies of the transmissions and a number of other technical details. They would also have to have the cooperation of the operator. Transmissions were sent by radio-telegraphy, and each operator—or "pianist"—had his own style of sending which was easily recognizable. The slightest variation could be spotted by an experienced ear.

From the beginning, the Abwehr had a hard time getting hold of these radio posts. The Gestapo was after the clandestine operators too, and generally stopped them before the Abwehr had time to intervene. Gestapo Chief Schreieder also planned to use the transmitters. In fact, he tried once, in January 1942, but without success. With the first transmission, the operator warned London that he had been captured. The transmission was cut short.

Hermann Giskes, therefore, had more than one reason for putting his scheme into action. First of all, if it succeeded, it would be an espionage coup.

Second, it would demonstrate the superiority of the Abwehr over the Gestapo.

This was the situation when Christmann's friend, George Ridderhof, entered the scene. Posing as a member of the Resistance, he had made contact with a network leader of the *Orde Dienst,* Captain van den Berg, and learned not only that *Orde Dienst* had good radio contact with London but that it was about to receive important agents and arms via a parachute drop.

Ridderhof at once warned the Abwehr and Giskes put his best radio-fixing experts in the field. Nothing. The radio had suddenly gone silent.

Furious, Giskes jumped on Ridderhof who could give him no explanation. But then, suddenly, Radio "Ebenezer" (its code name) began transmitting again. It had been damaged which had kept it silent for some time.

Now Giskes swallowed his pride and went off to visit Schreieder at his headquarters in Binnenhop to make a deal. They would mount an operation together to arrest the *Orde Dienst* radio operator. But the man would be left in Giskes' hands and "turned round" by him (put to work for the Germans). Thus began an operation which was to last two years—from 1942-1944—and known as "Operation North Pole" and "England Spiel."

On March 6, 1942, Giskes and Schreieder stopped the Ebenezer pianist, Hubertus Gerardus Lawers, in the middle of a transmission. Handed over to Giskes, Lauwers agreed to work under German control. He had been taught at the SOE operators' school that it was useless to play hero by refusing to talk; England did not expect that. The life of secret radio operators in occupied countries was difficult enough without asking them to make the supreme sacrifice. Therefore, an operator could give his code, frequencies, post —everything except his "security check."

The security check was a deliberate error in the Morse Code transmission. It was different for each operator. He transmitted it at set intervals during a transmission to identify himself. Failure to transmit warned the listeners, set up in an old house on the border of England and Wales, that the post had been captured and "turned." For Lauwers, for example, this security check consisted of an alteration of a sign every six letters.

The method had already proved itself. Another operator in Holland had used it with complete success. Unfortunately, since then—and without notifying anybody—the SOE had changed its mind about its reliability.

Someone at SOE had realized that the radio operators in occupied countries transmitted under extreme tension, in constant danger of discovery and often in very uncomfortable situations. This was spotted in the "touch" which was sometimes completely deformed, in the incomprehensible messages which were sometimes sent, and finally by the pianist forgetting to send his security check under pressure. The SOE people therefore decided that too much importance should not be attached to the absence or presence of the "security check," but they did not warn the radios already in operation of this change in procedure. They simply decided to "play it by ear," so to speak.

The result? Ebenezer was able to transmit for *two years* without ever transmitting his security check—and without anybody on the receiving end taking notice of it.

Lauwers, in fact, gave a false security check when Giskes asked him for it. In addition, he was able to fool his watch while transmitting and succeeded in introducing into several transmissions the following alert: "Captured and turned round, manipulated by the Germans since . . ." such-and-such a date. The SOE continued to have blind—and deadly, as we shall see—confidence in him.

Unfortunately, Giskes, who was only looking for a secret radio to manipulate, had stumbled into preparation for one of the biggest operations the SOE had ever mounted in occupied territory: the "Holland Plan." Ridderhof, when he passed on his information to Hermann Giskes, had not understood the importance of what he had discovered. He did not realize the arms and agents destined for *Orde Dienst* were part of a vast offensive. But, then, neither did Giskes.

The special conditions of climate, geography and strong Luftwaffe defense in Holland ruled out, Giskes thought, the possibility of an extensive armed Resistance operation in Holland. Besides, the military situation was changing swiftly on the continent. A new tension, an acceleration of the war, made the climate in the occupied countries even more oppressive—and dangerous for Resistance operations.

The Russians, since their entry into the war, had been urging the Allies to open a second front in Europe. It was the only way, Stalin said, of relieving the pressure on the armies of the USSR.

London, in response to this demand, had prepared Operation Torch, the November 8, 1942 landing in North Africa. It was not what the Russian High Command had in mind, but it was difficult for England to do any more. The United States, fighting in the Pacific and preparing for the African invasion, had not yet built up the war machine necessary to mount an offensive in Europe.

The British, drained after an exhausting year of supporting the weight of the European conflict, could not alone settle the war on the continent.

On top of this, Churchill had his own ideas about preparing for a landing in Western Europe. He considered it such a gigantic enterprise that he did not expect the first attempt to succeed—not without a deeper knowledge of the extent of the enemy's defense. The reports received from agents behind the "Atlantic Wall" were still too fragmentary, too superficial to give an exact picture.

Churchill thought it would be necessary to go through a sort of "dress rehearsal" before the general landing. A number of plans were studied with this in mind, most of which were abandoned.

There was, for example, "Operation Sledgehammer"—installation of a bridgehead in the Cotentin Peninsula (Northwest France, East of the Seine) which was abandoned for "Operation Jubilee" (landing of Canadian forces at Dieppe (on August 19, 1942).

The most ambitious plan of all was known as "Operation Roundup," built up on the following hypothesis: When the Allies landed, the Germans would voluntarily abandon France to concentrate their forces in the Low Countries and in Germany, in order to shorten their front and their lines of communication. The Allied strategy, then, would be a massive air attack on the landing coasts east and west of Le Havre, then a breakthrough in the direction of Calais, Antwerp, the Meuse, Belgium and Holland.

This plan, under serious consideration for some time, involved several complementary operations. The one which particularly interests us here was "the Holland Plan."

If the better part of the German army withdrew into the Low Countries, it was obvious that the decisive battle would take place there. The objective of the Holland Plan was to arm and prepare the Resistance to fight as a kind of "shadow army" behind enemy lines.

This presented many problems, the principal one being how to organize and arm guerrilla troops so far in advance of "D Day" without having them cut loose in premature actions; plus how to instruct them, command them, equip and supply them.

SOE, at first, considered asking *Orde Dienst* to supply most of the manpower for the secret army, because it was a para-military network whose members included a number of officers and non-commissioned officers. (It was also a "right wing" network of which the other networks were somewhat suspicious, but this did not interest the SOE). Support for this plan was even stronger after a visit to Britain by Lieutenant Gerare Doggers, adjutant to Colonel Schimmelpenninck, commander in chief of the *Orde Dienst*.

One can see that the Holland Plan was a far-reaching operation. It was, for a long time, the favorite of the British Army, notably of Field Marshal Sir Alan Brooke (later Lord

Alan Brooke). He attached so much importance to it that he suggested that the Low Countries should take over from France (the Resistance) the distribution of material and aid.

In March, 1943, the SOE received the following instructions:

"You are the authority responsible for the coordination of sabotage and other subversive activities, including the organization of resistance groups; you must furnish instructions and communications in all areas to the patriotic forces up to the time of their incorporation into the regular forces . . ."

Here we again find the germ of the permanent conflict between the SOE and the Resistance in the field: the SOE estimating its role to include not only the job of arming and equiping but raising, training and commanding the network forces; the Resistance groups, on the other hand, feeling that once the material and arms were in their hands they were quite capable of handling the rest.

What was more serious, however, was that the SOE received its instructions in such a way that it believed the grand European invasion would definitely take place sometime in 1943. Accordingly, it dangerously speeded up its part of the operation:

"The SOE will conform to the general plan by organizing and coordinating the actions of the patriots of the occupied countries at all levels. Premature revolts on a large scale must be avoided. The SOE must form and equip para-military organizations in the contemplated operation zones. The role of these formations will essentially be:

"To prevent the enemy from bringing up reinforcements.

"To interrupt enemy communications between the rear and the combat zone.

"To prevent enemy destruction of bridges, railway crossings, etc., likely to hinder the Allied advance.

"To carry out sabotage requested by the Allied command.

"To throw the enemy into confusion, notably by spreading false orders and rumors."

To accomplish this the forces were to split up in the following divisions:

    25 railway sabotage sections
    51 road sabotage sections

　　a number of communications and air field sabotage
　　sections
　　17 military zones

The first phase of these operations, decided on after the
SOE's London chat with Lt. Doggers of *Orde Dienst*, was to
drop instructors and radio operators with the necessary materials. Other drops followed—one of them the arms and
agents drop Ridderhof reported to Giskes.

So many parachute drops kept the clandestine radios very
busy and inevitably attracted the attention of the Nazi intelligence services. But even if Ridderhof had not managed to
penetrate the *Orde Dienst* network, the Luftwaffe, sooner
or later, would have discovered what was going on. Holland
was on the direct Allied bombing route to Germany and so
very closely watched that in the terrain—as pointed out
before—such drops were very difficult to hide.

Why, then, put the Holland Plan in motion at all? Why
was there such haste when the Allies preparing for Operation Torch knew they were far from ready to land in force
in Western Europe?

To placate the impatient Stalin? To throw confusion into
the mind of the OKW? To test the defense of the Atlantic
Wall? All of these reasons were probable. But the result was
so ludicrous and bloody that one cannot help thinking that
there must surely have been a better way.

But once the Holland Plan was set, it was necessary to
make the Dutch Resistants accept it, for they were to furnish the major part of the effort. The SOE had learned by
now that the *Orde Dienst* did not represent the majority of
the Resistance, but it had been in too much of a hurry to
deal with this. Now it was too late to think of gathering
together all the principal network leaders. They, therefore,
decided to air-drop a coordinator, a Dutchman everyone
would accept as their leader who would represent the government in exile and who would make all necessary de-
cisions on the spot.

For this task, the SOE chose Professor George Louis
Jambroes, a Master of Physics on the faculty of Utrecht,
who had fled to Great Britain in 1941 and who refused to
serve his country except in battle.

Word that Jambroes was coming was passed to the Re-

sistance reception company through—Ebenezer, in spite of
repeated warnings from Lauwers and other resistants that
his radio post had been captured.

With no effort on his part—without even realizing it—
Colonel Hermann Giskes put an end to the Holland Plan.
The Abwehr didn't know that it had disrupted what was
planned as advanced preparations for an Allied landing in
Europe; Giskes assumed they had merely "neutralized" one
more SOE attempt to organize the Dutch Resistance.

During this operation eighteen posts were captured and
turned over; fifty agents out of fifty-four were captured by
false "reception committees" as soon as they landed. Forty-
seven of these men—including Professor Jambroes—died at
Mauthausen. In addition, the Abwehr seized 570 containers
of material, 150 crates, 15,000 kegs of explosive, 3,000 Sten
guns, 5,000 light arms, 300 Bren guns, 2000 hand grenades,
75 radio transmitters, 100 signal lamps, three Eureka Bea-
cons, three Five-phones, 40 bicycles, and 50,000 pounds
sterling in florins; hundreds of thousands of pounds·sterling
in dollars, French francs and Belgian francs. This had the
disastrous long-term result of leaving the Dutch Resistance
without arms and supplies on the day when it was asked
to intervene for the liberation armies.

It was one of the biggest intelligence blunders of all time
and seemingly senseless, because Lauwers' heroic messages
had not been the only ones received in London by the
SOE.

On August 31, 1943, two captured Holland Plan agents—
Ubbink and Dourlein—succeeded in escaping from prison
at Haaren (a theological college in Brussels the Gestapo con-
verted into a prison). They took the road for England via
Switzerland · and after many mishaps arrived safely. *The
English refused to believe their story,* and they were shut up
in Brixton prison to silence their embarrassing revelations.

In November, 1943, there were three more escapes from
Haaren. Two of these agents stayed in the Low Countries
and sent their reports to London through a radio post which
had not been subverted by the Germans; the third agent went
directly to England.

The SOE did not believe these three any more than they
had believed Dourlein and Ubbink. Nor did they believe a

Canadian named Dessing who also aescaped from Haaren and made his report in England on September 3, 1943.

Finally, later in autumn of 1943, the Joint Intelligence Committee and the Dutch Section of the SOE, annoyed by the rumors of the terrible penetration of the Dutch Resistance and anxious to cover themselves, ordered an investigation.

The Commission's report, handed in on December 22, 1943, came to the following conclusion: "The functioning of the (Dutch) Section is satisfactory. A number of security tests have been carried out several times . . ."

Nobody talked, officially, about the Holland Plan fiasco after that, not until the end of the war. The British were content to modify the personnel of the Dutch section a bit and make it cooperate more closely with a new Dutch Service—the BBO—whose members, in London, included a number of Resistance agents escaped from the Low Countries. (And who, incidentally, were able to confirm what the SOE refused to believe.)

Nobody ever discovered exactly who was responsible for this intelligence catastrophe, nor how Giskes managed to keep Operation North Pole going for two years. In 1947, two years after the war ended, the Dutch government asked M. L.A. Donker to preside over a parliamentary commission investigation to find out who was responsible for the Holland Plan fiasco and the betrayal at Arnhem.

Donker's task was exceptionally difficult. For a start, the British War Office refused to let those responsible in the SOE testify. It sent two officers to The Hague who were ordered not to say anything and who performed this task perfectly. Nevertheless, some time later, with the agreement of the British Foreign Office, the Donker Commission came to England and interrogated a number of important members of the SOE. But the records were missing—destroyed in a fire in 1948.

So, no further light could be shed on either the Arnhem Betrayal or the Holland Plan Affair. Still, it was hard to believe that there was—in both cases—only stupidity or negligence to blame.

The case of Professor Jambroes alone, after all the importance placed on this agent, should have been enough to put the SOE on the alert.

Jambroes had, of course, been greeted by a false reception committee and jailed by the Germans in Haaren. But the SOE—thanks to Giskes—didn't know this and believed him to be hard at work "unifying" the secret army. Until Christmas, 1943, "Jambroes" managed to refuse successfully to return to London and make out a full report. Finally, at Christmas, the SOE refused to take any more excuses and delivered a particularly insistent order for his return. The professor finally agreed to oblige.

Preparations were made for Jambroes' return over Ebenezer radio. The return would be organized by the "Golf Team" which would parachute into Holland for the job. The members of the Golf Team were: Captain Krist, Lieutenant van Os and the brothers Pierre and Guillaume van der Wilder. They were dropped from a Whiteley on Feb. 18, 1943—right into the arms of the Gestapo!

But Giskes knew that he must organize the return of Jambroes—if his England Spiel operation wasn't to be blown.

A young officer named Karl Boden who spoke Dutch perfectly was chosen to play Jambroes. Since he was not too bright, he was given a guide to make up for his lack of intelligence—none other than our old friend, Henk Jandoel, alias Richard Christmann.

The pair made a "first escape attempt" which "failed" (naturally) in Paris, but gave Christmann/Jandoel the chance to make a few inroads into the "Reseau Prosper" and the "Vic Line" escape networks.

A second attempt allowed the false Jambroes to get as far as the Pyrenees. It finished with a car accident on the road between Tarbes and Pau—and the "death" of Jambroes. (The real Jambroes was shot by the Nazis in Mauthausen, in 1944.)

This was the end of the Holland Plan which had, by the way, existed only in the minds of the English and Colonel Giskes' false radio transmissions. It faded into oblivion.

Some said later that the Holland Plan was meant as a diversion to give "Operation Jubilee"—the commando landings at Dieppe—a chance. That it succeeded, because—thanks to the Holland Plan—at *Polizei Führer* Rauter's request three German divisions stationed in France were dispatched to the

Low Countries and three squadrons of Luftwaffe Hunters were to be diverted from the Ile-de-France and Normandy to Eindhoven.

But even if this were true, the unfortunate commando raid on Dieppe—on August 19, 1942—was a disaster. Out of 5000 men, only 2100 returned. The Allies eventually counted 882 dead, 587 injured, 1,431 prisoners.

For Christiaan Lindemans and others in the Resistance at this time, their lives were a nightmare constantly haunted by the fear of discovery and betrayal. Their best protected networks, safest sanctuaries, best kept secrets, all seemed to be known at Hermann Giskes' "Citadel" in The Hague. Friends left safe and secure one night might be prisoners of the Nazis the next morning. It was impossible to know whom one could trust.

For months, worried about the dangers Christiaan ran, his young brother Henk, and his childhood friend, Veronica, pleaded with him to accept their help. Finally, he agreed to set them up in a flat where he could sometimes leave fugitives from the Nazis in their care until he could move them along the escape chain.

Sure of their absolute loyalty, he set about assuring himself of their security. Nobody but he knew the address of the flat, nobody knew they were helping him. The escapees entrusted to his care and lodged there prudently ignored everything about them and hurried on their way.

Yes, Henk and Victoria were absolutely safe, Christiaan told himself. He believed it. Unhappily, he was wrong . . . and that mistake led him to the decision which was to destroy him. . . .

CHAPTER SEVEN

Scorching in June and July, wallowing in mud since October—Holland had never known such extremes of weather.

"Is it worse in war time than in peacetime, or does one only notice more?" Christiaan asked himself in an excess of gloom.

Wherever one turned, the news was bad. It was a nightmare to try and buy ordinary supplies. Everything was scarce: meat, butter, chocolate, tea, coffee, soap—everything except medicine, fruit and rotting vegetables. Now Madame Lindemans put on the table an ersatz coffee, no milk, a little piece of black bread and strange, sugarless jams.

It was not due to her lack of trying all over Rotterdam! Day after day, dressed in a shapeless skirt tailored in a material similar to sacking, with an old pre-war sweater and a very humble, ugly red coat (which, with a green coat just as ugly, seemed to have become the country's uniform) dragging along exhausted in worn-out shoes, blown up with the unnatural fat of an unbalanced diet, her shopping basket eternally on her arm, she waited in queues for hours in the hope of some unexpected distribution. She usually came back with an empty basket, but full of sad news gathered from the groups of housewives.

The Jews did not have the right to travel by bicycle or by car. They were periodically stopped. First they had been relieved to know that they were being interned in Westerbrook, in the Drente. After all, it was in the Low Countries. But then the BBC had called attention to the fact that it was a concentration camp as cruel as the others, and they lost hope.

The riots of young people against forced labor in Germany multiplied. One day, the Germans cordoned off an entire area of the city with troops and searched it, throwing into trucks all boys or girls old enough to work. Madame Lindemans was nearly taken in one of the scuffles. She just had time to take cover in Henk Jandoel's shop.

Her son Christiaan's friend had been charming, full of attention, even offering her a small glass of gin to comfort her. She was still trembling! Henk Jandoel was a good boy, friendly, intelligent. She was proud that Krist had such a good friend. She had hurried home to talk about it, to tell everyone what a marvelous friend Krist had. She wanted to show that he was not an impossible boy at all, that he had very understanding friends.

Christiaan had gone to the railway station. So many things were being said that he wanted to see for himself. He saw long lines of young people "requisitioned" for work inside Germany, herded like cattle into the railway carriages.

As a result, there was a mass escape. How it was managed was never disclosed. The railway employees had been "overwhelmed" and the Germans had arrived too late.

In retaliation, the Germans shot a group of hostages. This provoked interminable discussions between those Dutch who blamed the Resistance for such reprisals and those who thought that it was right to save the young people from forced labor.

Christiaan had no doubt about what was right. The Dutch *should* stop the young leaving, not only in their own interest but to deprive the Germans of this labor. That was the infallible criterion, that which should always come first: what made things most difficult for the Third Reich? In this case, things were made doubly difficult because shooting the hostages turned the population against the occupier and brought him nothing.

Christiaan lived by his "golden rule": deprive the Germans of all they needed. He brought back to his mother whatever he could find that she might be able to use or barter: candles, soap, ration cards, coffee, sugar.

"Take them, Mommy, take them," he insisted when she hesitated. "It is better for this food to go to good Dutchmen than to the Germans."

"But you need it for your *onderduikers*," she objected.

Christiaan smiled. "Don't worry—they lack nothing. We have our methods. The air raids are not for nothing."

After each RAF bombing raid, in fact, the special documents—ration cards, identity cards, etc., which were absolutely necessary to exist in occupied Holland disappeared from government offices.

Still, the Resistance effort was not enough. The towns were sad. Very young children wandered the roads, some bone thin, others swollen with the watery gruel that was now their "basic diet." They nibbled sadly at bits of carrot or bread . . . but what bread!

In summer and winter alike, they wore wooden clogs and were often without shirts or coats. They hesitated to go home where there was no light at night, no fire in the winter, where in any seasons they might return to find the doors bolted, the house deserted and their parents taken away by the green or black military cars which patrolled the towns and villages day and night.

Christiaan had retrieved three such very small children whom he had found in tears and confusion. Their mother had gone shopping and had never come back. Their father had been taken away practically under their noses. Fortunately, Christiaan discovered, they still had some family who took them in.

Every day stories were told of children left orphaned, of students jailed for having refused to bow to the German masters. Every day Allied planes attacked port installations, air fields, and factories. Every day the sky was filled with the deafening thunder of bomber squadrons in flight, followed by the flak and—less and less often these days—by the Hunters of the Luftwaffe.

All this was the daily bread of the occupation, the back-cloth of life in Holland.

About the activities of the Resistance, opinion was becoming less and less divided. Church leaders dragged the reluctant along with appeals such as this:

"Dutchmen! Do not remain passive. Fight as best you can —in your town, in your own way—for liberty, for the country, for the people and for religion. Give what you have, help without reservation."

Appeals were so widely heard that Anne Frank wrote in her *Diary:* "It is not really the fault of the Dutch if the Jews go through so much misery."

Christiaan was called on more and more by the various Resistance groups. Workmen, students, Jews—the number of *onderduikers* increased. It was necessary to get false papers, to find hiding places and especially to find them work with sympathetic employers, for the best way of escaping was still to change one's identity.

Everybody was at it. A ration card cost as much as thirty Dutch florins, but certain bakers supplied food free of charge —without tickets—to those who were in hiding. Certain Resistance groups energetically ransacked the distribution services of those in charge of supplies and the offices of civil status. Such raids, scrupulously timed, quickly executed, were the type of expedition in which Christiaan excelled.

Basically, the operation was simple. A small band of resolute youths were divided into four sections. One, the army, protected the operation and called upon the employees of the center in question (civil status or supplies) to put their hands in the air and to be quiet. That was easy; the employees had no intention of holding up the operation. Another group watched the doors to frustrate troublesome intrusions. A third filled large bags with the wanted documents. The fourth group consisted of the drivers who waited at a distance in their vans, the motor running, ready to make a quick getaway as soon as their friends returned—mission accomplished.

Christiaan once took part in an even more elementary operation which needed only two men—himself and a friend. The employees of the supply depot had alerted the Resistance in advance that they would find their ration cards on a certain day and hour on a small, low table away from the center of activity. All Christiaan and his partner had to do was pick up everything and disappear. Nobody saw anything . . . or did not want to see anything.

Adventures of this sort were the good side of the secret life. Like the reunions of friends, discussing about operations, the travel and sabotage orders. The bad side were the enemy counterattacks of England Spiel and other network penetrations.

Suddenly, arrests took place one after the other. Men disappeared. Others reappeared horribly mutilated, swearing that they had said nothing, betrayed nothing, betrayed no one. Nevertheless, the Gestapo continued to strike sure, direct blows. Other disappearances took place. Their comrades did not know whether the resistants had been arrested, or whether they prudently had simply taken off, left their homes, decided to no longer frequent familiar haunts. This was better than those who returned to a rendezvous apparently free but actually followed by Germans in civilian clothes, ready to round up anybody seen in conversation with their "suspect."

The escape networks particularly were going through a tragic period. In Stockholm, the sector was fairly calm, but the Pyreenean line seemed to be plagued with strange incidents. Christiaan could no longer set out on his missions without anxiety.

Gilou Lelup had written him, putting him on his guard. Paul (Jandoel's friend) had disappeared some time ago. She was not very upset, because she had not liked him at all, but his disappearance seemed to have been the signal for a giant wave of arrests. Christiaan had already been aware of this: he had heard of it from his contacts in the Pat O'Leary network.

People from "Prosper," "Pat," the "Vic Line," "Dutch-Paris" and from a few other networks more or less related to these had been arrested. There had been raids on houses of refuge; agents who were thought to be perfectly camouflaged had been taken in the shadows. The Nazis seemed to be very sure. Someone had betrayed the resistants!

Christiaan felt the danger without being able to guess where it was coming from. It was unnerving.

"You were really part of the Van den Berg group?" he asked Ridderhof one day. "He was taken in one go, I was told."

Ridderhof hunched his shoulders and remarked evasively: "For the short time the war lasts, we will all get through you know."

Christiaan did not pursue his questioning. He did not remark on the fact that Ridderhof seemed to be the only member of the Van den Berg network still at liberty.

For a few days, nevertheless, Ridderhof watched "his friend Lindemans," asking himself how much the young man knew. But, at length, Ridderhof felt reassured. Decidedly, Krist was only a poor fool, a dissipated young man and a terrible smuggler—nothing more.

Jandoel mentioned Paul's disappearance to Christiaan one day:

"He left on a journey and never reappeared in the north. Do you think something could have happened to him? You haven't heard anything during your travels have you?" he asked.

"But of course not! How do you expect me to know about such things?" Christiaan replied. "I don't know him as well as you do, and I have no special means of information. You know me . . . the Resistance stories, I don't understand much about them."

Had Jandoel-Christmann believed him? Probably, for neither he nor Ridderhof questioned the young Dutchman further. They showed no more interest than usual when, in December 1943, Christiaan announced he was leaving on a trip.

"I am going on a tour of Belgium and France. I must pick up a bit of money," he explained, "otherwise my mother will have to forget a New Year's present."

The Abwehr was deep in the destruction of the Holland Plan at the time, and Jandoel and Ridderhof had other things to interest them.

Christiaan left to escort a friend anxious to put distance between himself and the Gestapo.

The friend was Kas de Graaf, a tall man with brown eyes and regular features who looked like a British officer in a Guards Regiment. He was brave, with a gay courage, a lively sense of humor, very warm-hearted. For a long time he had played a very active role in the Resistance and, as a result, had now become dangerous to his whole network. The Germans were so interested in him they had started to watch his family. It was time to leave.

Quietly, methodically, he organized his departure. He hoped to find some friends in Paris who would put him on the road to Spain, but he needed a guide for the first part of the journey. He thought of Christiaan, whose services he had been using for other escapers since the beginning of 1943.

On the tours the two men had made together, Kas de Graaf had become attached to the tall young man who was at once simple and complex, brutal and gentle. Now they discussed their coming journey.

"We will stop at Lille," said Christiaan, who wanted to see Gilou Lelup, "where we will try to get news of the situation in France. How far do you want me to accompany you?"

"Oh, no further than Paris," Kas told him.

"Perfect. That will allow me to return here and spend the New Year with my family."

The two left a short while before Christmas, at the moment when the occupation authorities announced a special distribution of 250 grams of butter for the end of the year celebrations.

"Happy celebrations!" commented Christiaan wryly. "Who would have thought we would still be at war in 1944!"

It had been raining steadily for days. The roads were slick, shining and black, without lights. Passersby hurried along, for no apparent reason. Nothing good awaited them anywhere. Neither in the empty shops, nor in the houses without heat, nor in the restaurants and cafes . . . icy, inhospitable, or else full of Germans and collaborators. They hurried, out of habit, to escape. But escape from what they did not know. Perhaps the enemy who was always on the lookout for "idlers."

It was no better at Lille where Gilou and Christiaan's little girl charmed Kas de Graaf. The news was not encouraging. Always the same thing: arrests, disappearances, raids, abductions, torture.

"One no longer knows whom to trust," concluded Gilou

"I'm glad you two are going on from here to Paris in one go. It is much better."

They arrived, in fact, without mishap at the *Gard du Nord* in Paris. Here, they separated.

"You are certain you no longer need me?" asked Christiaan.

Kas de Graaf shook his head. "No, now everything will take care of itself. Thanks, old man. See you soon in London. You have been working around here too long. You should take a bit of air too."

"Bah," Christiaan retorted, "Not yet in any case. I hope never. I have my habits, you know."

Kas de Graaf did not insist. He understood the feelings of his guide. "In any case, we will see each other again, Krist. Don't make any mistakes, eh?"

"No, you neither. And if you need me again, remember that I shall be in Paris for a while. A message at the Montholon Hotel will always find me."

Kas smiled. He knew that Krist was making the most of his travelling to renew his female conquests, or make new ones. "Visiting the personnel of the network," he called it.

But the following days were for Kas de Graaf a series of frustrations. The doors on which he knocked did not open or were half-opened and a fearful face whispered a few words and then disappeared behind the suddenly shut door. He was unable to arrange a rendezvous, or to make his contacts. The passwords were repeated by speakers who did not seem to understand their meaning.

Throughout the city the situation had become strained. The Nazis, angry at their losses on the Eastern front, were cracking down on the resistants with a vengeance.

Kas de Graaf finally exhausted not only his ingenuity, but his money. He had got to the point of considering returning to Holland, when he thought of Krist, who might not have left Paris yet. He went to the Montholon Lafayette Hotel, a small building, in a quiet road where they agreed to take a letter for Christiaan.

The next day the two men met. Krist, smiling, dragged his boss towards a safe house, in the Neuilly area. A young girl received them, asking no questions, seeming to find the situation perfectly normal, giving up her room without hesitation to the travelers.

It was late. Kas de Graaf was exhausted. He went to bed and fell immediately asleep. But even so he slept lightly. A slight noise, merely a sigh in the air, and a ghostly light, were enough to wake him a few hours later. He lay motionless a moment, eyes shut, imitating the slow breathing of a sleeper. Then he opened his eyes.

Christiaan Lindemans, dressed, was sitting at a table, the only light a minute piece of candle. He was laboriously tracing characters on a piece of crumpled paper with a little bit of pencil which was almost completely lost in his enormous hand.

Kas de Graaf shut his eyes again, then overcome with curiosity, he sat up in bed.

Christiaan lifted his head. The two looked at each other in silence in the pre-dawn gloom.

Kas saw then that his companion's face was wet with tears.

"Krist! You are crying! What are you doing?"

"I thought you were asleep."

"You woke me up," Kas said.

"I'm sorry. You need rest. We have a hard journey ahead of us. Me, I was writing to my old mother. It's—it's not funny."

Kas de Graaf, touched, tactfully changed the subject. "Why do you say *we* have a long journey to do?"

"Because I must come with you. You have found no one here."

"But I can still find—"

Christiaan shook his head. It was too dangerous, he explained. Kas was lucky not to have stumbled across a traitor ready to turn him over to the Gestapo. He could not stay in Paris any longer without attracting attention. And Christiaan knew the way. He had his personal relays at Bordeaux, Dax, Peyrehorade. He did not even need to ask General Martin, who was in charge of a Spanish Republican network, for a mountain guide. Krist knew how to reach the frontier as well as any of them.

Kas let himself be convinced. It was obviously the least dangerous way.

The two made an uneventful journey through France. Eventually, they arrived in the heart of the Basque country, not far from Saint-Etienne-de-Baigorry, in a forested region of mountain passes with surrounding peaks reaching a height of about 1,400 metres. In the good season, the journey would not have presented any difficulties, but it was the middle of winter and the mountain streams had frozen in their beds. They could not follow them without making an infernal noise and risking breaking their necks. They could not count on the noise of the running water to cover up the sound of their passage. Neither, if they came across a patrol with dogs, could they hope to give the animals the slip by walking in the water. Everywhere nature was hostile. They risked their lives with every movement and were frightened of losing their bearings. Traveling on foot, skis, or with snowshoes, they could not help leaving very visible and very dangerous traces behind them.

They therefore decided to go through the woods as much as possible. They climbed in silence, trying not to make any noise, trying even to control their breathing. Suddenly Christiaan stopped: "We're being followed. It was too good to last."

"You sound as though you were expecting it!" Kas said.

"In the last village—I didn't want to say anything to you—but I noticed somebody was very interested in us—in that café. He must have given the alert."

What had the man seen? What had he guessed?

"It may be a shepherd," suggested Kas de Graaf, without believing it.

In the middle of the night, a few hours before Christmas, it did not seem probable. With luck, it could be a smuggler who would not betray them. In any case, it was too late to turn back. They had to go on, towards Orbaiceta, in a direction parallel to the Iraty mountain river. Kas recalled hearing of escapers who had passed on skis, in the middle of the day, in the middle of a crowd from the winter-sports resort, but he had chosen another way and he must stick to it.

He looked at his guide who whispered: "Continue without stopping whatever happens, but softly. Head straight on."

A dark blur moved between the trees.

"Is he alone?" Kas asked.

"Of course, of course, don't worry, walk!" Krist ordered. Kas had not the slightest wish to obey. Christiaan hid as

est he could. Kas took a few hesitant steps, then imitated
his friend. He could not let him face such danger alone.

The man approached them, menacing, a revolver in his
hand. He shouted something they did not hear. First he saw
Christiaan and then Kas. He stopped, hesitating, wondering
which to go after first. Krist made the most of this to jump
the man and throw him on the ground. With powerful hands
he gripped the enemy's neck.

The silence of this savage fight had something horrifying
about it. When everything was over, Christiaan got up slowly.
Kas joined him and helped him search their victim. The man
was carrying a Gestapo identity card. The snow was falling
quite steadily and soon it would bury him.

"You should have fired," Kas said. "He was going to."

"And start an avalanche with the shot? Anyway, noise
travels too far in the mountains," Krist said.

The two fugitives continued their journey. Suddenly, Christiaan stopped. He pointed out the icy bed of a large mountain stream.

"The Iraty," he explained. "Follow it to the first big village,
that will be Orbaiceta. Spain starts here. You no longer need
me."

They looked at each other without saying anything and
tried to smile. Then they shook hands, still in silence. Emo-
tional display was not for them. They had succeeded. Christiaan had completed another crossing: for a friend in battle,
a friend and a chief. What was there to say?

Kas de Graaf descended towards Spain. Between him and
freedom there was still the possibility of French prison, but
however unpleasant one might be did not involve torture and
execution.

Immobile, indifferent to the cold, Christiaan watched his
companion move away. He could have followed him, but
he did not even think of it. The road to Spain he knew by
heart. He would take it one day, when the time was right, but
not before.

Like all guides, all "frontier ferrymen," he had come to
the very edge of security, and voluntarily turned his back on
freedom, retaking the road of shadows and horror. Of all the
types of courage tested during the Resistance, none was more
extraordinary than that of the escape guides.

Actually, there was a time when Spain did not seem a very desirable haven. Before the Allied landing in North Africa, before the Russian offensive, no one could know what fate Franco reserved for fugitives. But now it was Christmas, 1943. The caudillo of Spain knew perfectly which way the war was going. There was no longer any question—even though "German commissions" always ploughed the country —of delivering resistants to the Nazis. Spain had become the giant step toward freedom, the great temptation. Christiaan Lindemans refused to succumb to it. They were waiting for him in the north. He turned back alone and returned to Paris.

Usually, when in Paris, he liked to go to The Montholon Hotel, with its ridiculous little square and its stones celebrating the virtues of the Catherines. He liked the girls who welcomed him and who patiently listened to his talk.

But this journey, Krist did not feel like enjoying himself. He did not know whether he would ever see Kas de Graaf again. He found himself thinking of all those in the Resistance who had fallen. There were so many. Strange premonitions came to him then. He tried not to take them seriously but they irritated him immensely.

He hoped for some comfort from a visit to an ugly middle-class house in the rue de Vaugirard, but he was disappointed. Here he met Victor Zwaan, father of one of his couriers, Elly Zwaan, and adjutant to Doctor Maurice de Voss. Helped by Christiaan, this little group controlled a tributary network of Dutch-Parish. The conversation, as always, turned to a certain number of "packages" waiting to take the road to Spain.

Christiaan expressed his fears to Zwann, who had no patience with them—or him.

"It all depends on you," he said harshly. "Nothing will happen if you respect the security rules a bit better. But, if you continue as you are now, one day the Gestapo will plant a woman of whom you will not be suspicious and we will all be taken."

"There is no danger of that," retorted Christiaan. "I do not confide in them. Presents, yes . . . and . . . you can guess what I mean. But in love or not, sober or not, I do not talk. Never. I have a greater sense of security than all your cool middle-class types put together!"

Zwann did not believe it. Later, he was to tell the head of
Dutch-Paris, Jan Weidner, "A boy as immoral as Christiaan
could not serve a great cause." Zwann did not like him and
would have liked to have kept him at a distance. But it was
not the moment, because he needed Christiaan to get more
money from Dutch-Paris.

Doctor de Voss's little group had terrible money problems.
Evidently, Dutch-Paris could fill the till, but it was necessary
to persuade Jan Weidner to agree to it.

"I have arranged a rendezvous for you with Weidner,"
Zwann told Christiaan at their next meeting. "He has good
contacts in Switzerland with our embassy. He receives quite
a bit of money and can easily set us going again. Naturally,
the best thing would be to persuade him to let us merge
with Dutch-Paris. But if that doesn't work, make sure our
subsidies are restored at least."

"What type of man is Weidner?" Christiaan asked. "I think
it would have been better to entrust your mission to someone
other than myself."

"Who knows our problems better than you?" Zwann
argued. "As for Weidner, well, his father was a Protestant
minister. He is a Seventh Day Adventist, he is also non-
violent and he has friends in the RP Chaillet group—you
know, the Jewish-Christian Friendships."

"And you are counting on *me* to make a good impression?
You have funny ideas around here. I bet he takes one look at
me and goes away with the offended look of a housewife
who has discovered a cat has peed on her door mat. But, all
right . . . how do I recognize him?"

"The rendezvous is in a cafe, and I thought it would be
simpler if I came with you as I know you both."

Krist sighed and nodded impatiently. "All right, but don't
make me late. I have a train to catch to Rotterdam."   -

Zwann promised that the interview would be brief. He did
not think of asking Christiaan, who normally liked to linger
awhile in Paris, what was so important in Holland? It was
unfortunate, because then he would have known that the
young man had just heard of the arrest of his brother, Henk,
and the girl, Veronica, by the Gestapo!

Christiaan volunteered none of this. He and Zwann left

together, Christiaan, as usual, armed to the teeth—which
would not make a good impression on Weidner.

The discussion was lengthy and Christiaan was in a hurry
because his train would soon be leaving. He ended up by
asking Weidner to continue the conversation on the way to
the station. Finally, an agreement was reached. Weidner
would immediately furnish material aid to the De Voss network. (Subsequently, he had to renew his subsidies.)

But he had seen enough of Christiaan who seemed to him
"an imprudent and violent adventurer" who "could not have
been taught any morals" as he "liked women and even mixed
with those of debatable virtue." However, moderating this
somewhat rigorous moral judgment, Jan Weidner adds today
that King Kong had "a good heart," an active desire to help
others—especially those who were being persecuted by the
Germans. This must be remembered, because it partly explains the misfortune which eventually befell the young
resistant.

In the train going north that January, Christiaan cried. He
had promised to protect Henk and Veronica. That promise
was broken, and they were going to suffer because of him.

Henk was only a child, a boy who had grown up too fast
in the hardship, the ruin, the suffering of war. What would
the Gestapo do to him? Krist knew only too well! The
thought of his baby brother's frail body undergoing torture
made him grind his teeth. And Veronica! Devoted, tender,
gracious Veronica . . . "interrogated" by the Gestapo.

Oh, they would not talk, of course—which made it even
worse. They would never talk, whatever was done to them.
This was why he would have to be the one to get them out
of it, wrench them out of the grasping claws of their torturers.
He would do it. He alone could do it.

He must return to Holland . . .

There must be people alive today who know what went on
in Christiaan's life between the day he learned of the arrest
of Henk and Veronica and the day when he agreed to go to
Brussels to keep a fateful rendezvous with Colonel Hermann
Giskes. But if there are any, they have kept silence.

Christiaan was courageous and easily touched by the mis-
fortunes of others. But he was also impulsive, bad-tempered

d "immoral," they said, because he liked women too much.
: had few friends, few influential friends. Kas de Graaf
s far away now; he could do no more for Krist.

He was a confused, unhappy man, half mad with grief,
:apable of reasoning clearly, ready to clutch at any straw
hope, anything that would save Henk and Veronica.
He was ripe, in fact, for the unscrupulous.

The Abwehr, thanks largely to England Spiel, had poisoned
many networks in the Netherlands that the Dutch Resis-
nce groups no longer knew where they were at. It was im-
rative that they retaliate by infiltrating an agent into Colonel
skes' organization. A "double agent" who would tell such
plausible story that the Germans would swallow it com-
:tely. But a double was needed who could be sacrificed
need be—if the operation went wrong, or if his services
:ame useless; a double, therefore, who could not boast of
ving many influential friends.

And then Christiaan Lindemans came to them with his
oblem, the anguish there to read in his eyes. Of course the
:at, soft-hearted "King Kong"—braggart, woman-chaser,
ol—was a natural for the role, the horror of which he did
t suspect. He only understood one thing: only the Ger-
ans themselves could save Henk and Veronica. At the same
ne, his leaders pointed out, he would be saving the lives
hundreds and hundreds of resistants . . .

How could he refuse? Henk and Veronica, condemned by
German tribunal, already awaited execution. Neither of
em had talked, though Veronica had a broken arm and
r nails had been pulled out. And they were going to die.

Christiaan accepted the "contract," with misgivings, and re-
rned to Rotterdam. Taking a thousand precautions so as not
betray himself, he went home when night was falling. The
rage was dark, deserted. In the house, in spite of the black-
t, he could distinguish a faint light, No fire, though, with-
t a doubt. Christiaan shivered in the shadows. Perhaps he
s wrong to come home?

Nevertheless, he rang the bell—his particular ring—and
ard his mother coming quickly, lightly to the door. His
ther loomed behind her as the door opened. They sur-
unded Krist, kissed him. They had had no news from him
r so long!

He asked: "And Henk?"

"You knew? He is still in prison."

He saw the despair in their faces, felt their anxiety. must stop; it hurt him too much. He stroked his mothe hair and said: "We'll get him out."

"Krist, you're mad! It's not possible! They'll take you well, that's all you will gain by it." She began to cry.

He threw his shoulders back then, pretended a confiden he did not feel. "I know what I am saying. Everything ready. We have our plan. The English are marching with m We could empty that prison and all the prisons in Hollan but we won't do that—it's not the right moment. But He will come out, Mummy, I promise you. Don't cry anymo you mustn't cry. You must have confidence. I'm not scar . . . it is the Germans who are scared of me. They ha nicknamed me 'King Kong,' because they think I am a ki of superman. It's stupid, isn't it?"

Not at all convinced, Madame Lindemans murmure "Krist, oh Krist, my son, be careful. What are you going do?"

An annoyed gesture, as if fighting off a fly. It was startin again! It was unbelievable—they still had no faith in hi All he had suffered, accomplished, it was nothing. He r mained Krist, who only talked of doing great things. P tiently, he said, "Don't try to understand, Mummy, it is to dangerous for you. Believe me, have confidence, don't a any questions. Henk will come, here, soon . . . with Veronica

He asked, after a brief silence: "This evening, Mumm can I sleep here?"

"Of course, my son. You are home. You are staying then

"No, but I will come back. I would like to see my broth first. He still lives near the port? In his little house with h little wife?"

Yes, he had to see his big brother. He had to justify hir self for having exposed Henk to danger, tell him that Her was going to escape, thanks to him and him alone.

His brother greeted him coldly as if he did not know wh it meant to Krist, this terrible arrest!

He listened in silence, consulted his wife with his eyes b fore answering, refused to believe that Krist could do an thing and overwhelmed him with reproaches.

Why was Krist not in Holland when Henk was arrested? Where was he? On a mission? Really, how easy it is! They knew all about them, his missions: one day of work and ten of debauchery! Meanwhile, Henk was in the Gestapo's hands, "interrogated," and they knew what that meant. But Krist, where was he?

Krist lowered his head in silence. It was true that Henk had admired him, had blindly followed him. Everything was his fault, he realized it! He was guilty, the unbearable little boy that his brother scolded, the black sheep of the family!

For a moment, he believed it. Was it true? Perhaps he was a failure, as his brother maintained. Perhaps there was no glory, no "King Kong" legend.

The two brothers looked at each other in silence. They had the same blue eyes, the same massive build, though Christiaan seemed bigger.

"Don't say that," he murmured. "Don't say I'm a good for nothing. You complain because I was not here when Henk was arrested—which means that you needed me, that you knew I could save him. And I'm going to!"

"But, of course," his brother answered with weary irony. "You are going to make them open the prison doors for you, and perhaps stop the execution at the last minute, like in an adventure story?"

"You don't understand! We *live* in an adventure story we *onderduikers*. Henk wanted to share that life with me. He did. I will save him."

He was getting excited now.

"Henk will be free!" he shouted dramatically. "Or we will die together."

Moved in spite himself, his brother asked: "How will you do it?"

"Don't worry about that. Stay nice and quiet in your little Resistance office!"

He got up, pushed back the table blocking his exit and left, slamming the door behind him, leaving his brother and sister-in-law anxiously discussing the situation.

Krist would go home now, in the middle of the night, despite the curfew, because all such stupid little regulations were not for him. He was too strong, too powerful to bow down to them. He abandoned the others to their tight little moralistic world. Perhaps he was a good for nothing, as his brother claimed, but, nevertheless, he would be the one to free Henk.

It was pleasant in the dark, deserted town. Damp and cold, but pleasant. The silence was soothing. The darkness was good for one. He could hear the patrols from afar and prudently took cover. It was easy, in this universe of ruins, easy in the black-out. It was enough to stop for a second, to stoop a bit in order to blend into the background of the "hollow country" that Rotterdam had become. Krist laughed silently joyfully, his gripping his revolver, thinking about the Pyrenees, the Gestapo agent and Kas' escape.

Back at his parents' house, his father was already asleep, but his mother was waiting for him, like she used to when he got back late and often drunk. But that night it was not alcohol that made his eyes bloodshot, that made him frantically kiss his mother. It was a relentless resolution only expressed by a murmur: "Tomorrow . . . tomorrow. . . ."

No more was needed to exorcise the horrible vision of Henk and Veronica awaiting death in their prison. The die was cast. Krist could not back out now. Henk and Veronica could only be saved by him. They would be.

His head under the covers, so as not to see anything, hear anything, he trembled at the thought of what lay ahead. But in the morning, his resolution had not weakened and he was calmer. He reassured his mother, and drank a cup of real coffee: "Where did you get it, Mummy?"

She smiled feebly, her mind full of terrible foreboding, and replied; "We still had tires to trade." Then timidly, she added: "Krist, don't go . . . stay here . . . you will all die, Henk and you. . . . Henk will not be saved, but you. . . ."

He got up to stroke the trembling shoulders fondly. He murmured: "You know very well that everything can be bought these days in Holland. Don't be afraid, Mummy, it is only a question of money. And we have some. The Resistance has. . . ."

She would have liked to talk, to ask questions, but she could see in his eyes that he was already far away. He squeezed her against him to make her be quiet, lifted her effortlessly, kissed her and promised her again that Henk would return.

"I may have to disappear for a while, but you mustn't worry about it. All is arranged. Nothing will happen to me. And even from afar, I will always think of you, be following you, protecting you."

She watched him go. As the door closed after him she murmured a prayer. Christiaan did not hear her. He was off to keep his fatal rendezvous. He had reached the point of no return.

CHAPTER EIGHT

"We have received reinforcements." A friend from his Resistance group was bringing Christiaan up to date on events in the Netherlands during his absence.

Indifferent, eaten away with pain, thinking only of Henk, of his promise, of what he would have to do to keep it, Christiaan absently asked, "Yes? Who?"

"I don't know. I haven't seen them. Five men from London. Boys from home that they have released in the middle of the Wieringermeer Polder—you can imagine the picture!"

"It's better to land in the marsh than to fall straight into the welcoming arms of Schreieder, and that at least proves that all of our networks aren't rotten. But you don't know any more?"

"No. Except that their leader is clamoring for you. He says he knows you, needs you, and will only go via you."

"He knows me . . . there are five of them . . . they need me."

As if in a dream, Christiaan repeated that to himself, thinking of the uses to which he could put a reinforcement of five Dutchmen, trained in London, strong, armed, with funds probably. What more could one ask? With "five cavaliers" he would have all he needed to rescue Henk. Perhaps, after all, he would not have to go through with his terrible mission. But would the others agree to help him. Aloud he asked:

"How can I meet them?"

"You can't. It seems that London has given them formal instructions. They should only contact you through a circuit-breaker. But if you want my opinion, it will be quite soon. They were very impatient to see you. You'll just have to wait."

Wait! It was easily said. In his prison, Henk also waited—for death!

At last a liaison agent met him, fixed a rendezvous, explained that a guide would show him where to meet his contacts.

These people from London were very careful. Still, there was no reason to complain about that. After all, they had made enough mistakes; it was time they began to see sense.

The liaison agent was unknown to him. He also talked a lot. Krist hardly listened to him. Only one thing counted for him: to meet the leader of the expedition.

Finally, a rendezvous was set, and Christiaan discovered that famous "Boeschauten" he had been hearing so much about was, in fact, an old friend: Bob Celosse. He was discreet about his mission, insisted on the security precautions that had been imposed on him in London.

Christiaan immediately told him about Henk. The two friends sauntered through the streets talking quietly, calmly, as though it were peacetime. To see them, one would have taken them for two companions calmly discussing a holiday project.

Celosse, especially, was worried: "We can't," he said regretfully. "Not before a certain time, and then it will be too late. You understand."

Yes, Christiaan understood. Celosse was a brave man. If he had been able to, he would have mounted an operation against Henk's prison, but, for the moment. . . .

Christiaan yielded. It was destiny. There was nothing one could do. He was alone, as his superiors had told him. No one else could free Henk for him.

By the time of Henk's arrest, England Spiel had caused enough havoc for the Dutch as well as the English to make them start asking themselves questions.

Of course, it would have been childish to expect the SOE

to plead *mea culpa*, admit its blunders and agree to a clean sweep. But it was obvious that something was amiss with the Holland Plan. Sending in control teams was a desperate solution that could cost them a number of valuable men. This is why they thought of using the services of a resistant to infiltrate the Abwehr, as near as possible to Colonel Giskes.

The most difficult thing, naturally, was to find the man, the double agent who could possibly be a hero after the war, but who could be sacrificed without regret if it was necessary. As Pierr Nord indicated in *"Mes Camarades sont morts"* (written under his real name of Colonel Brouillard): Nothing is as difficult to solve as the problem of recruiting a double, especially if one has decided to prefer a patriotic man to a professional man.

The first is much better than the second, but "if people with high morals exist who have become doubles, it is nevertheless not a career to be recommended. It is a profession which, one way or another, always turns out badly. A job where one way or another, nine men out of ten turn out badly. One has to be an angel in order not to dirty oneself. There are a few angels on earth. Very few are available for the special services."

Most patriotic doubles are *not* angels. They are "romantic, imaginative, excited. They are legion, their driving power is infinitely less solid and durable."

Christiaan was one of these: a romantic, an impulsive person, who would perhaps "not last" very long. But one who could be persuaded to play this dangerous game by telling him first that it was the only way to save his young brother's life and, second, that he would be able to make his mark in the Resistance, that only he was capable of playing this role—a role out of the ordinary, the role of an archangel with a blazing sword!

Of course, Christiaan's superiors, before throwing him to the lions, took care to give him a little course in the use of patriotic double agents. This could have discouraged him, and they risked not being able to find another candidate of his quality, one whom they thought of as "expendable," but it was a calculated risk.

This may seem cynical, but the leaders of the special services were conditioned to cynicism by their very positions.

And the amateurs, having entered the profession during the war, seemed to go even further along these lines than the professionals. Spying is a job which corrupts not only the agents but, perhaps even more, those who manipulate them who end up becoming cold, unrelenting monsters.

Poor Christiaan instead of being put on his guard received a sort of "pep talk" meant to excite noble sentiments. The only warning he received was half-hearted: "If an accident happens to you, we can't do much for you. You will have to count on your own ingenuity."

Armed with this, he left Rotterdam one morning in a wheezy little train with wobbling carriages which were going to sway all the way to Brussels.

Finally alone, a victim of the inaction of the journey, he had nothing to do but think. He thought of Kas de Graaf whose advice he would have liked to have. He thought of Henk and Veronica. He thought of his mother. Reluctantly, he thought of double agents he had known whom he had always avoided. Contemptible people with shifty eyes!

Oh, of course, he was not like them! He did not sell himself to have a foot in both camps. He was acting under orders, but, still . . . how did one recognize a "good" double from a bad?

The express reached the black smoky arches of the Brussels station. Slowly it stopped by the platform. A compact crowd stepped down from the carriage, a much larger crowd than one would have believed possible looking at the car. Civilians, laboring men mostly, mingled with soldiers of the Wehrmacht. The workmen had gray complexions, threadbare clothes.

They were coming from the Atlantic Wall bunkers, from air fields, docks, arsenals. A crowd of profiteers, with their heavy rings, arrogantly pushed and shoved, overperfumed, over made-up ladies in tow wearing too many jewels and furs.

Everyone intermingled, shouted at each other, sometimes even helped each other before spilling out of the entrance to the station, lost in the traffic and the pedestrians. Christiaan followed this human tide, taking big strides, isolated because of his height and his thoughts.

Now that he had arrived, he asked himself where and how he was going to contact the Abwehr. Nobody had told him, because he had boasted of being able to join "the leaders of the German secret services" his own way. Truthfully, all he knew was that the Abwehr had a few offices at the Metropole Hotel. He could not see himself asking advice from the porter or the reception desk!

He hesitated, slowed down, was pushed by passers-by. It was drizzling. He shivered, pulled up the collar of his jacket, told himself he had had enough of wandering about the streets. In any case, and before attacking the enemy, he needed somewhere to hide, where no one would know anything about him, where he would not risk compromising his network friends. For the first time, then, he realized how very alone he was. Him, King Kong, roaming about Brussels looking for a resting place!

Suddenly, he had a marvelous idea. Mia Meersmans! Why not? They accused him of liking women too much, but women were sometimes very useful!

Mia, a ravishing Viennese girl, lived in the Hotel Cosmopolis, and she maintained close relations with the SD. What was even more interesting was that she believed that Christiaan did not want to get mixed up with the SD. What did she know about him? He had often wondered. He had introduced himself to her as a black market dealer and she had pretended to believe him, but was she taken in? Or had they given her orders to watch him? Did she know he was in the Resistance? That he was the great King Kong?

He hesitated. More than one network had suffered because of such a situation. But after all he was on his guard, the game of hide-and-seek that he had between Mia and himself gave spice to an otherwise dull adventure. Besides, Mia had a lot of friends. Margarethe Albrecht, for example, an SD agent with whom more than once Christiaan had also spent an active night, but who frightened him a bit and whom he normally preferred to avoid.

He found Mia in a crepe de chine combination, in the middle of making-up.

"I wasn't expecting you!" she said distressed. "And I've already arranged to go out!"

In fact, laid out on the bed as though lying in state was a black silk dress, a fur coat, gloves, a hat and a bag. On the carpet next to the bed were a pair of high-heeled shoes.

Krist held the girl round the waist with one hand while the

other fondly caressed her small bust. He bent down, breathing in the perfume of her body. He ran his lips along her neck, lingering in the hollow of her shoulder. Mia trembled.

Krist," she said quietly, "we shouldn't—look at the time!"

He looked at nothing, but he freed Mia.

"You're right. We will see each other later. This evening. Can I come here tonight?"

"Late, then?"

"Very late, I promise."

She smiled. Neither of them had any illusions.

"I must meet some friends first. About some tobacco," he told her.

"Well, you see? Everything will work out fine."

He sighed. He was less certain about that. But, anyway, he had a bed for the night. Mia pleased him, she would ease his frayed nerves.

Mia finished dressing. Krist waited for her. They left together but quickly parted in the street. She must have been heading for a bar quite near, for she did not seem dressed for a long walk.

They made an odd couple, she very elegant and he dressed in an imitation tweed jacket and grey flannel trousers and without an overcoat.

He walked in the direction of Rogier Square. He had had an idea. He knew two men, Dutch like himself, but living more often than not in Brussels, who generally took their evening aperitif at the Hotel des Grands-Boulevard's café. Their names were Anthony Danen and Cornelis Verloop. Krist did not like them at all, but they would be useful to him. They worked for the Germans, that was known. Were they pure and simple traitors or double agents? Christiaan had never found this out. He thought that it would be quite ironic if they were playing the same game.

But this was not important. The essential point was that Cornelis Verloop could put Christiaan in touch with Colonel Giskes. But, would he be willing to? Probably only if Christiaan seemed to him to be a suitable recruit for the Abwehr. It would not be easy. He would have to work hard to convince this man. On the other hand, he must not overdo it or Verloop would become suspicious.

Henk, his younger brother, had been taken by the Gestapo,

also Veronica. They had been condemned to death for sheltering escaped English pilots. How could he save them? Christiaan was at his wit's end. Would Cornelis be able to give him advice? Tell him who to see? He would do anything, absolutely anything, to obtain his brother's pardon.

Yes, it would be all right. Cornelis Verloop was not overly intelligent. And since the story was true, as far as it went, it would not be too difficult a part to play.

It was pleasant in the café, sealed off from the outside by heavy curtains. There were a lot of people there and lights, a lot of lights; it reminded one of peacetime. Really, in Brussels, one was better treated than in Holland. The occupation was less harsh. This struck him on each journey. He weaved his way between the tables, at first dazzled by going into the bright light after the darkness. His eyes quickly became adapted and he saw Cornelis Verloop sitting alone. Good! It was what he had hoped for. He approached and flopped into a nearby seat.

"Is anything wrong?" asked Verloop after a brief look at his drawn face.

"You must help me . . ." Krist began.

"If I can, old man, of course!"

The false cordiality of the traitor made Krist feel sick, but then, he thought, wasn't he nearly as bad. In a dull voice, he told the story of Henk.

"He worked for the English?" asked Cornelis.

"Yes. You know, he's only a child. He did not understand what he was doing!" Christiaan said desperately.

"Of course, of course."

Cornelis was quiet, listening attentively. He was not sure that he believed Krist—the story did not quite ring true. Henk would not have worked for the Allies without his brother's approval. Therefore, Krist must have been an Allied agent, and he had come to him because he knew Cornelis was a German agent. Krist and he had known each other a long time, but this was the first time that either of them had alluded to their undercover work. It was difficult. They did not dare advance too much. Nevertheless, they had to find a way to prolong their discussion.

Finally, Krist admitted: "I've had enough. Everybody has deserted me. I must save Henk—I don't care about the others. You must arrange a meeting for me with the head of German espionage here."

Cornelis raised an eyebrow. "How you carry on! And then?"

"I know you can help me. But, don't forget, I need someone important, someone very important—the underlings don't interest me. When he knows what I can do for him, he'll give you a decoration for having brought me to him. I promise you," Krist told him.

"But—" Cornelis got no further.

"Now, no stories. You know who I am. Surely you realize that I'm offering you the chance of a lifetime?"

Unconsciously, Krist had taken up a commanding tone. Men like Cornelis had to be handled firmly. The cudgel—he would understand that.

Cornelis yielded: "If I do manage to arrange a meeting, how can I get in touch with you?"

Christiaan was exultant. It worked! Verloop was trying to make him give an address. Luckily, he had his answer prepared.

"Here will be perfect. A large café with noise and a lot of people. The ideal place where we'll not be noticed."

"You can't leave mail here," Cornelis objected.

"Who's talking of writing? That's the last thing I intend. No, I'll pop in every day—at midday, three o'clock in the afternoon and six o'clock in the evening. When you have arranged a rendezvous, come and tell me. Yourself. If you send someone I don't know, I'll refuse to make contact."

Cornelis was visibly disappointed. His superiors would have only his word. He was bringing nothing tangible. No address, no mail, no contact—nothing! He could only say one thing: a chap he knew, Christiaan Lindemans, wanted to work for the Germans. He had worked for the Resistance. He would have something to tell. Really, it was little. But Christiaan was adamant, sitting with his arms on the table, looking at him intently. Finally Cornelis answered: "As you like. But I can't promise you anything, you understand."

"I understand. Nevertheless, I advise you not to fail me."

Standing up, Christiaan signaled to the other to wait, not to follow him, and then let fly a parting shaft: "I leave you with the bill."

Cornelis blushed, furious. By the time he had collected the bill, Christiaan would be far away. He slumped back into his chair, looking after the slowly disappearing young Dutchman.

Outside, Christiaan hesitated. He had no more to do, no one to see. He would find a restaurant and kill time until it was time to join Mia. Suddenly he felt empty, anxious. Tomorrow, or the day after tomorrow, Cornelis Verloop would introduce him to the Germans, and he would have left a whole period of his life behind him. Silently he prayed that at least Henk would be freed. Otherwise he hated to think what would happen. The idea that the Abwehr might trick him made his heart swell with rage.

His superiors had told him: "Be careful, the Germans are as intelligent as we are. You will not be accepted straight away. They won't believe you. You can only hope to succeed in the long run. Be patient. And don't forget we don't want to hear from you. Now, what will you tell them . . . ? That you have served us faithfully. But we can do nothing for you, or for your brother. It's too much, the cup is full. You have changed sides and chosen the Abwehr. Not the Gestapo, because they are brutes (and because they do not interest you) but Giskes. And don't forget to be remorseful. You are going over to the enemy, but you don't accept just any work. It's very important, if you want Giskes to have confidence in you. . . ."

They had forgotten one thing, these Machiavellian leaders. That was to warn Christiaan that if someone from his side accused him of treason, nobody would lift a finger to help him. Indeed, they would plunge him in deeper, if it served their purposes. . . .

CHAPTER NINE

Colonel Giskes was at Dreibergen when Captain Wurr telephoned him from Brussels to ask him to come and deal personally with an important and delicate affair.

Since 1941, when he arrived in the Netherlands, the situation had changed for Hermann Giskes. The defeats undergone by the German army on all fronts had reflected on the reputation of the Abwehr. Admiral Canaris and General Oster, and a number of their officers, were accused of wanting peace at any price and were in disgrace—or worse. Gestapo boss Himmler made the most of it by extending his empire and asking that the complex services overlapping the Abwehr be attached to him.

He seemed to have obtained, by the end of 1943, a favorable decision—in principle—for the following year. But, warned in time, Giskes had worked out a counter plan. He proposed that the services depending on him at least—i.e., counterespionage in Belgium, in the Netherlands and Northern France—be made into a new organization, the FAK 307 (*Frontaufklarungskommando* 307) which would be directly attached to the QG 111 West in Paris.

In this new set-up, the QG and FAK 307 would be settled

in Brussels, with "stations" in Lille, Antwerp, Gand Luttich
and Dreibergen. This transformation, backed by the commander-in-chief West and by the OKW section in charge of
military information on the enemy armies, would be concluded in April, 1944.

In March, Giskes had only a few rooms in the Metropole
Hotel and a base in the Botanical Gardens. Soon he hoped to
be allocated more important officies in the Place de L'Industrie
(FAK 307 would settle down there only to leave ahead of the
Allied advance. It would then settle successively at Roermond,
Bredon and Schloss Hillerath near Bonn). Thus, its name
camouflaged to keep its independence, the Abwehr IIIF continued to work as best it could, although its influence and its
activities were considerably limited.

Ironically, about the time that Christiaan's superiors decided to infiltrate Colonel Giskes' services, those services were
losing their power and their efficiency. Christiaan's mission
was actually useless! The Abwehr, at the beginning of 1944,
was in no position to start again—or even to back up—an
operation like England Spiel. Its actions against the Resistance
movements would, from now on, be sporadic, badly coordi-
nated and ineffective.

On the other hand, if the Dutch services of London, the
SOE and the English military were interested in finding out the
extent of England Spiel's damage, they already had in their
hands statements and files enabling them to reconstruct the
situation and to fill in the gaps.

Colonel Giskes immediately realized how useful his pros-
pective new recruit could be. If Christiaan was as well known
in the Resistance as he claimed, he could perhaps supply them
with the essential information that the OKW clamored for:
the date and place of the Allied invasion of Western Europe.

He could thus become Colonel Giskes saviour. For such
information would certainly pardon him for having worked
under the disgraced Canaris. In this period of internal strife
in the German services, when a man could easily end up in
prison or dead, this was an unexpected chance for Giskes to
save his long scrawny neck.

Therefore, as soon as he arrived in Brussels from Dreibergen, he went straight to the Metropole, where he immediately
recognized the pink face and fair hair of his favorite adjutant,

who was absorbed in eating his midday meal in the pseudo-oriental dining room.

Captain Wurr explained, over lunch, that a man known to the Abwehr by the code name of "Nelis," lent to Brussels by the Lille station and specializing in the penetration of networks, boasted of having caught a choice piece of game: Christiaan Lindemans from Rotterdam who claimed to have occupied an important post in the Allied network.

Nelis (Cornelis Verloop) had brought him along the previous day to the Botanical Gardens and Wurr, an old hand at his job, had been very impressed. Wurr was of the opinion that either Lindemans was the mine of information for which FAK 307 had been searching, or they were dealing with an exceptionally dangerous double agent.

Wurr had avoided answering when Krist asked him if he was in contact with the head of German counterespionage. He wanted to see "the boss" and no one else, Christiaan insisted. Anything else would just be a waste of time for everybody.

Wurr had asked him to give some samples of the information he was able to furnish. Submitting to this preliminary test, the young Dutchman had quoted names and networks appearing in the secret files of the Abwehr.

"Really?" Giskes asked doubtfully.

"Yes, really!" Wurr nodded eagerly. "For example, he says he is in contact with the CSVI of Amsterdam and with the Financial Organization of the Resistance. Well, he proved it to me by naming the man in charge of the Paris section. This seemed important enough for me to decide—without consulting you—to arrange a meeting for this evening at 1800 hours, and for me to promise that this time he would actually meet you."

"What is he like?" Giskes then asked.

"He's a giant. He combines brutality with an almost childish simplicity. Nelis confirms that he really is a unique personality. He also says that he has often fought with the German police—for he is also a saboteur. He shoots first and asks questions afterwards." Wurr laughed. "He has been nicknamed 'King Kong' and he has, in fact, something gorilla-like about him. I would not like to stand up against him. One feels he is unpredictable and dangerous. In short, my Colonel, he frightens me. I would like you to meet him yourself."

"Who will attend our meeting, besides King Kong, you and myself?"

"Willy and Nelis," the captain said. "Nobody else. The less who know him, the better it will be."

Giskes nodded. "I intend to arrive a bit late—don't be surprised. There is no harm in making him wait. It will relax him!"

It was about 1830 hours when Colonel Giskes made his entrance at the office in the Botanical Gardens. Four men were already sitting around a table. Three stood up at the arrival of their leader. The fourth remained seated, yet he seemed to be a good head taller than the others.

Wurr had not exaggerated, Lindemans was a giant with a child's face. He seemed about thirty years old. Giskes introduced himself, using the name of "Gerhardt" (according to the tradition of the information services which demanded that one use various assumed names beginning with the initial of one's real name).

Everybody sat down. Christiaan stared at the newcomer in silence.

"Can you explain to me your presence here?" asked Giskes, to start the ball rolling. "They tell me you are in contact with the enemy services. That is not sufficient. Who are you? What do you want from us? What can you offer us in exchange?"

Christiaan answered in German:

"Are you the leader of German counterespionage? He alone can help me and I refuse to waste my time talking to someone else. What you need to know about me, I told yesterday to M. Walter [Wurr]. My name is Christiaan Lindemans. I come from Rotterdam, and I haved worked for the Allies since 1940. Six months ago, at my request, my youngest brother agreed to help me to ensure the escape from Holland of some English pilots shot down over our country. He was captured. The Gestapo handed him over to the German military tribunal which condemned him to death. As it was I who involved my little brother, I feel responsible for him. My friends all say that they can do nothing for him. But if you managed to free him, I am prepared to tell you—in exchange—all I know about the Allied services. I know the whole Resistance from the North Sea to the Spanish border like the back of my hand.

In five years, I can assure, I have had time to learn a lot! But I will only talk under the following conditions . . ."

Christiaan leaned forward, eyes on Giskes. "I know that the Abwehr does not resort to the same tactics as the Gestapo, which is why I came here. I don't want you to arrest *en masse* all the friends I name, and I insist that those who are taken be treated humanely. But what will determine everything for me will be what you do for my brother. If you give me your word he will be freed, I leave the rest up to you."

He put his fists on the table, enormous fists, like sledge hammers, and looked at the German with an extraordinary intensity. His steely blue eyes riveted Giskes.

"I don't know what has happened to your brother," Giskes began slowly, "or which hornet's nest he is in. But if he is charged with nothing other than having facilitated the escape of some enemy pilots, I think I can promise you his freedom."

The colonel paused, then said, "As for the other, you are quite right to think that the Abwehr is not interested in massive persecutions. Our practice has been to watch and eliminate the network leaders when necessary, to 'turn them' to find out London's intentions. What I do, therefore, will essentially depend on the value of your information."

There was a long silence then during which Christiaan examined Giskes, as if he wanted to read his mind. Finally, he got up and strode up and down the room in a state of extreme agitation. He seemed to open his heart, not to his new allies, but to some distant judge, invisible and severe.

This attitude was not completely put on. Christiaan had been under extreme tension since he had accepted the formidable job of working as a double. Henk's destiny, on the one hand, had upset him deeply; on the other hand, up to the last second he had been unsure of how Giskes would react to his proposition.

In five long years, he had acquired a certain respect for the German services and was not at all under the impression that they were easy to fool. He could not know, of course, the changes which had shaken the interior of the Nazi war machine, or Giskes' need for a reliable informer. Now that he was so close to his objective, Christiaan was not at all sure of success. So, he launched in the following monologue:

"For five years I have thought only of one thing and that

was of how I could help the Allied information services with
all my strength, with all my energy. I did not ask for thanks
or rewards, but only came across ingratitude, suspicion and
treachery. You cannot know how many ambitious and collab-
orating vermin have become rich thanks to the Germans and
are now hurrying toward us because they think your defeat
is near. If you can imagine it, you will understand me better.
You will understand better my reasons for coming to you."

He paused for breath, then went on.

"The men with whom I have fought since the beginning of
the occupation are no longer there today. They are dead, missing or in prison. Only a handful of friends remain in whom I
dare have confidence. God spare them! What I can tell you
about London's projects and those of the Resistance is far
more important to you than the capture of a few men whom
others will replace immediately and, besides, who won't talk.
Just give me back my brother and I will allow you to do what
you want with me. They call me 'King Kong.' I don't do
things in halves. I am the friend or the enemy of men, depending on the way they treat me. I would like, from today, to be
one of your friends. I have always been told—and I have
always believed it—that those who work honestly for you
are decently treated. I want to deserve your confidence, for I
have enough experience of information to know that one
cannot give one's confidence in halves. It's all or nothing in
our work. I only want to show what King Kong's friendship
is worth and what he is capable of."

This little speech had deeply moved its deliverer. At times,
Krist even managed to believe what he was saying. He had
followed the instructions of his superiors who had advised
him to let his imagination run freely, for one is only convinc-
ing in one's own way. Therefore, at the end of his monologue
Christiaan was nearly as moved as he seemed to be. He strode
to the table and, grabbing his large briefcase, emptied it with
a theatrical gesture.

Giskes and his aides examined the contents of the case
spilled on the table. There were complete files of various
documents: questionnaires, circulars, white identity documents.
There were official seals, rubber stamps, facsimiles of German
official signatures. A 9mm pistol; packets of French, Belgian

and Dutch bank notes. One of these interesting samples would have been enough to send the holder to a concentration camp.

Christiaan seemed to conceal with difficulty a certain pride in the display of so much proof of his secret activities, and also satisfaction at the surprise his "new friends" were unable to hide. Especially interesting were documents relating to the Organisation Todt (civil engineer and construction battalions) and to the Wehrmacht. There were travel permits with stamps, signatures, registration numbers. The only thing missing was the holder's name.

Giskes and Wurr made a few imprints with the rubber stamps, and Giskes appropriated an Organisation Todt circulation permit, intending to have it examined by the responsible authorities for a security investigation. Meanwhile, Wurr was taking note of document serial numbers.

Christiaan, visibly satisfied with the impression he had created, packed his samples back into his briefcase. Giskes could have asked why he was replacing so carefully the files and packets that he had just undone, where this material had come from and where Christiaan was now going to take it. But he did not. His doubts had melted like snow in the sun. Few resistants, he knew, could produce at once so many valuable documents.

He contented himself with saying: "I have no advice to give you, but be careful, nevertheless. I would be sorry to lose you, now that we have met, for I think you can be very useful to me."

At the same time, he suddenly realized that Nelis was still there and he was annoyed. Why had he not thought earlier of dismissing him? Nothing he and Christiaan Lindemans had to talk about was any business of this minor agent. After all, the man belonged to the Lille section. Giskes hardly knew him.

Nelis (Verloop) was asked to leave, just when he was starting to congratulate himself for having brought Christiaan to the Abwehr and calculating the reward that he could ask!

He left, annoyed that Christiaan had been witness to his humiliation. At the time, the incident passed unnoticed. But, later, it was to have formidable consequences. Verloop never forgave Giskes or Christiaan.

"You must have a code name," Giskes said when the door

had closed behind Nelis. "Your name is Christiaan, so we will call you 'C.C.' "

He went on to explain to Christiaan that he would be his "practicing officer," that Wurr and Willy would be his contacts with the Abwehr, that he should entrust himself to no one else. Then he gave him the most thorough interrogation.

By nine o'clock that night, Krist was stretched to his limit, worn out. He made the excuse of an urgent meeting in order to get out. He needed to think, to ask himself if he had really succeeded at the first meeting in gaining the confidence of the head of counterespionage for the OKW for Northern Europe.

He was wrong, by the way, to have the slightest doubt. Giskes, himself, realized later that he was completely won over that night and quite proud of having enrolled an agent of such importance at a time when people no longer wanted to serve Germany!

Christiaan walked, carrying his briefcase, in the dark and deserted streets of Brussels, where the silence was broken only by the stomp of the patrols and rumble of Allied planes on their way to bomb Germany. He dragged his legs along, worn out but triumphant. He had deceived the Abwehr! He had obtained Henk's freedom and Veronica's. He had kept his promise to his mother. He had won!

But of course not, he suddenly thought, with a tightening of his heart. He had only won the first round. Everything still had to be done. Giskes had asked him to draw up—with the help of Wurr and Willy—a complete account of his Resistance life. The colonel had not tried to hide that he expected him to penetrate all the networks still active in the Netherlands and learn for him the date and place of the Allied landings in Western Europe. Only that!

For the first time, but not the last, Christiaan was frightened. He wondered if his superiors were aware of the hornet's nest they had put him in, and if they would furnish what was necessary.

Suddenly, he began to walk faster. He was hungry. He needed to forget this evening, forget everything. Besides, he really *was* supposed to meet a contact, whom he found at the appointed place waiting for him, grumpy and impatient.

"Here you are! You took long enough!"

Christiaan shrugged. "Giskes kept asking me questions. I could not leave him earlier."

"It doesn't matter, as long as everything is all right," his contact said. "You don't need the briefcase anymore?"

"Certainly not! Go on, take it, put it back in place. Only two or three papers are missing—Giskes has them. Now . . . goodbye. I'll make my report tomorrow. This evening, someone is waiting for me."

He headed for the Hotel Cosmopolis. Mia, he knew, was having a few friends in. A night of drink and love, this was what he needed to forget the meeting at the Botanical Gardens and the fear of tomorrow. . . .

The next day, a session began which was to last for seventy-two hours! Christiaan talked, Willy took notes, Wurr asked the questions. Then Willy typed out Christiaan's report which he reread and made a few changes in. Nobody slept, they hardly took the time to drink very strong coffee, eat sandwiches and have a shower. At the end of the third day, Wurr finally decided he was satisfied and announced that he was leaving for Dreibergen to deliver the report to Colonel Giskes.

What was there in Christiaan's report? According to Giskes, he gave an exceptionally precise and detailed picture of the underground activities in Western Europe. Escape networks, houses of refuge, passwords; the means of renewing a lost contact, of replacing an arrested agent; the ways of reaching the frontiers; names and pseudonymns; information concerning the financing of the resistance; the contacts with London, the help to threatened agents. The whole mosaic of a "revolt" the size of which the Abwehr had never guessed was drawn for the astounded head of Abwehr IIIF.

They could not verify everything for fear of "burning" this new and promising agent, but everything that could be checked was—and turned out to be accurate. Now Colonel Giskes did not have a shadow of doubt: Christiaan Lindemans was the man he had always dreamed of contacting. He *was* the man he claimed to be, Giskes was sure of that.

It was, therefore, absolutely vital to obtain Henk's and Veronica's release to insure C.C.'s continued valuable cooperation. One morning the two youngsters suddenly and inexplicably found themselves standing outside their prison in the weak sun of Rotterdam. The wind stroked their faces, made Veronica's blond hair blow. The nightmare was over for them. They were free.

Meanwhile, Christiaan's report passed from hand to hand in the different sections of the Abwehr. Giskes stipulated that the source of this information could not be revealed and that nobody in it could be arrested for whatever reason without consulting FAK 307, responsible for handling the agent to whom they owed this marvelous harvest.

Captain Richard Wurr had taken the young man in hand and was giving him his agent's education, convinced that only a "classical service" can make good spies. Once in a while, Hermann Giskes sat in on the lessons. Not to watch over Wurr, for he had total confidence in him, but to show Christiaan the value attached to his instruction. This, he thought, must flatter C.C., and he took advantage of it to launch into a speech he had prepared a long time ago for a turncoat Allied agent:

The war should not degenerate into the savage butchery invented by the sadists of the SOE. They put in danger the innocent—women, children. They lit the fires of civil war and revolution, stirring up hatred, legitimizing crime. Giskes himself did not want that. He had fought unceasingly to make such enterprises fail. Now he was relying on Christiaan to help him protect Holland.

The young man listened, nodded his head approvingly. He was not there, after all, to contradict his mentor. They had explained to him that the Abwehr only asked one thing of him: to play his role as a resistant, to be up to date on everything, watch over everything—and wait for the most important task.

At this time, the discovery of the date and place of the Allied landings in Europe was the essential information wanted. It took priority over all else for the German information services in Western Europe. The German high command would need to have military superiority at the time of the landings to push the invaders into the sea before it was too late. The OKW reasoned that Allied attack must be pushed back within three days—or else. They had to have the information at any price. The enormous air superiority of the Allies could annihilate the defensive efforts of the Wehrmacht. If it became necessary to move up reserves, disaster could reult; the same if they made a mistake about the probable anding place and it was necessary to transfer troops in a direction parallel to the front.

In this situation, what did they expect from Christiaan?

All French, Belgian and Dutch networks had been warned that, at the time of the landings, they would receive the order to go into action in "personal messages" broadcast by the BBC. Naturally these messages would be drowned in a sea of other messages. The German listening posts already devoted most of their time to recording these messages and trying to penetrate the code. How much easier it would be to get the information from the Resistance. Giskes hoped that C.C. would unlock that secret.

It is necessary to repeat that Christiaan never gave the Abwehr that information. That,s as we have seen, he did not betray the plan for freeing Antwerp.

Christiaan Lindemans was a traitor—or he was a "good" double, a "patriotic" double following the instructions of his superiors. Giskes, as seen from his memoirs, liked to stretch the number of his successes and did not voluntarily admit to having been fooled. He only admitted it when it was impossible not to.

CHAPTER TEN

"The life of a double . . . is more dangerous and, especially more depressing than that of a simple agent," Pierre Nord has written. "One thinks one is covered by both sides. Illusion is quickly shattered under the gaze of one or the other."

It would be difficult to summarize better the essential core of the cruel ordeal which awaited Christiaan. Four years of secrecy, four years of being close to—and often fully aware of—the deception of other double agents had not been enough to make him see what he was getting mixed up in. Only after he was in too deep did he realize the danger, but then it was too late to turn back.

He had exhausted himself trying to convince Giskes that his conversion to the German cause was sincere. But other ordeals faced him. For example, despite Giskes's promise that none of the resistants named in Christiaan's first report would be arrested, two raids had been made by the Gestapo.

The reason for this breach probably lay in the backbiting which was going on between the German services. But Christiaan, drowned in a new world of deceit, saw it as a trap, a sadistic test thought up by Giskes.

Afraid, angry, disappointed, a victim of two camps, a pawn

of events, obliged to sometimes wonder whether his sacrifice was the slightest bit useful, Christiaan searched in vain for peace of mind. He took refuge in the company of women and drink, the only remedies he knew for torment, a balm which became less and less effective.

He was restless, welcomed any change with relief. He was delighted to learn that they needed him in Belgium to collect and deliver arms that were to be dropped by parachute in Holland for the Dutch Resistance.

He notified Giskes who saw in this proof of his confidence in Christiaan. He also saw it as a fine example of how slow English Intelligence could be to react.

Giskes had always maintained good relations with the Luftwaffe and was kept up to date on all the movements of the British "Moon Squadron," in charge of supplying the Resistance.

Both the Abwehr and the Luftwaffe got something out of this arrangement. Thanks to the "turned" radio posts, Giskes knew about the parachute drops several days in advance and he could alert the Luftwaffe.. The RAF supply bombers were allowed to reach their DZ (drop zone) but were attacked on the return journey. In two years of England Spiel twelve planes were shot down during 200 sorties, a much higher percentage of losses than over other occupied countries. Giskes, by the way, had been worried that this would alert the SOE to the England Spiel operation. Actually, it was not until March 1944, that it decided to divert operations to Belgium, where the sky appeared less unhealthy. The RAF attributed this solely to the fact that the Luftwaffe was specially active in the Netherlands because it was on the bombing approach to Germany! The SOE had absolutely no suspicion that anything else was responsible for its losses.

Relieved at the idea of a change of air, Christiaan moved in with Mia Meersmans at the Hotel Cosmopolis. His main reason was that it was not easy to find a bed in Brussels, a town which valued German officers highly. But another reason was that solitude of night had become intolerable for him. He needed noise, movement, new faces. At Mia's there was always something going on, and nobody noticed his comings and goings. As long as he returned with his pockets bulging with money (thanks to the Abwehr) full of vivid stories of black-market trafficking, they asked no questions.

He was beginning to get adjusted to things when suddenly his life was shaken by a tragedy for which he never forgave his superiors.

During a journey to the Netherlands he met a friend from the Resistance who asked him to help with two escapers from Haaren who were trying desperately to reach England.

"They are real patriots," the friend Jan Nauta, said. "You cannot refuse them your support. They are in grave danger, but no one in England seems to realize their plight! So far nothing has been arranged for them."

It was, Nauta knew, an appeal which Christiaan could never refuse. In fact, he immediately agreed to look after the two, but insisted on meeting them personally beforehand. Those concerned found that perfectly natural. It would delay their departure, but, as they remarked: "Since our escape has been put off for so long, one day more or less makes no difference."

The two men concerned were Jan Rietschoten and Aast van der Giessen, MVT agents dropped by parachute, in June and October 1942 respectively, straight into the arms of Schreieder from whom they had eventually escaped.

Jan Jacob Rietschoten, student at the Technical College in Delf, had reached Great Britian with a group of friends in September, 1941, by crossing the North Sea in a row boat —which was quite an exploit! In June, 1942, as part of the Holland Plan, he had been dropped by parachute near Assen. The Gestapo had picked him up, imprisoned him in Haaren. There he eventually met a young marine officer, Aast van der Giessen.

When they heard of the escape of two of fellow inmates, (Ulbrich and Dourlein) in August, 1943, they decided to try their luck.

Their prison was an old theological college four floors high, requisitioned in the summer of 1941, by Schreieder to hold political prisoners.

The place stank of disinfectant and crucifixes decorated the white walls. The men were held in twenty cells on the second floor, three to a cell. They were able to make contact with each other in the interior of the building during the communal exercise, and therefore, were able to communicate with each other quite easily.

The bolts on the doors and the bars across the windows were not too firmly fixed. Also there were too few guards. The Germans were, in fact, obliged to appeal to the Dutch Nazis for help in manning the prison. The Dutch were not very happy about the job. In such an atmosphere, one can see the possibilities for escape.

After the escape of Ulbrich and Dourlein, the Gestapo took particularly strict precautions inside the prison. Armed German sentries constantly patrolled the perimeter, which was further protected by reflectors, flood lights and an imposing network of barbed wire. In addition Schreieder relied on the effect of fear.

Every Monday and Friday afternoon the Germans lined up Dutch hostages or political prisoners in the ancient garden in front of a firing squad. The victims invariably faced death with dignity, while their friends sang patriotic songs at the tops of their voices.

It was from this prison that Rietschoten, van der Giessen and a third prisoner, Anton Wegner, escaped during Christmas 1943.

The success of the exploit was mainly due to Wegner, a shy, unobtrusive young man who wore glasses and whom the guards considered a timid soul. He was put in charge of little maintenance jobs, which allowed him to secure a small saw which he hid in his clothes. With this tool, the other two conspirators cut a trap door in the ceiling of their cell. Other prisoners kept watch while they worked, covered up the noise from the saw and helped mix the plaster which hid the hole from the Germans.

When everything was ready, the three friends climbed up through the trap-door into an attic which was used for storing junk. They pulled apart the bars of the skylight and slid down a rope, made of old laundry and rags, to the ground.

It was icy cold and black. Rain was falling—penetrating, never-ending. The sentries, discouraged by the weather and convinced that the night would certainly be quiet, had taken shelter. Once in a while, one of them would wipe the steam from the window with his hand and peer out into the dark, hostile night. No one missed the three prisoners until the following day. By that time they were already far away, hidden in the world of *onderduikers*.

They had, in fact, been told that if they could reach the Ijzeren Man Inn, in Tilburg, they would be taken care of by one of the networks which would hide them temporarily in the Van Leeuwers' farm. From there, Anton Wegner, who had a contact in the escape line, headed straight for England. Rietschoten and van der Giessen (by now known as Aas van Krimpen and Jan van Rossum) decided to stay in the Netherlands.

When they asked to be put in touch with a radio operator, they were sent to one belonging to the "group Heintje." Thus they were able to inform London of their adventure, asking for instructions and offering to pursue the work for which they had been parachuted into Holland. At the same time, they sent a long report on their capture, their escape, a list of the inmates in Haaren and also a list of the eighteen secret radios parachuted into the Netherlands which had been "turned round" by the Abwehr and were now serving Giskes' England Spiel.

To their great surprise, nobody seemed to attach the slightest importance to their revelations. They thought that their message had not been understood. They decided that they must return to Great Britian and personally tell them how the Holland Plan was—or, rather, wasn't—working.

They asked for a submarine pick-up. They were told that was out of the question but that England would try to send a motor torpedo boat to the coast of Walcheren. A "personal message" on the BBC would inform them of the departure time.

This message was never broadcast. Instead through agent Jan Nauta, the two agents were put in touch with Christiaan. Christiaan listened to their story, was convinced of their good faith and suggested that he contact London himself via an operator of his who was at Berg-op-Zoom, in Holland. If he could not arrange a pick-up in the near future, he would take the two men across by the Spanish route.

He asked Rietschoten and van der Giessen for identification photographs so he could obtain the necessary travel

›cuments: a special pass for Zealand, which was a forbidden ne, and frontier and dividing line passes in case they had turn off the Spanish route.

Equipped with these photographs, Christiaan asked his rect superiors for the necessary documents, informed them the situation and his own intentions.

His superiors had a Machiavellian idea: they advised him show the photographs of the two escaped prisoners to olonel Giskes! When Krist balked they explained the beauty the operation: Of course, Giskes would immediately cognize Rietschoten and van der Giessen, but he would ot feel like arresting them again. On the contrary, he would delighted to play a trick on the Gestapo by allowing the vo agents to get away. Giskes knew that Schreieder was arching for them, furious at having been tricked.

Christiaan was not convinced: "I can't see the reason for lling Giskes. On the contrary, I can see the danger of involving him."

"The reason is to consolidate your position with the bwehr," they told him. "Your warning constitutes excellent formation' with no danger to anyone—believe us!"

In the end, Christiaan let himself be won over. He needed s superiors to obtain the necessary travel permits, and he ould always abort the mission if Giskes did not react in a tisfactory way. He could hide Rietschoten and van der iesen for a while, then send them to Stockholm.

At first, everything seemed to work out as his superiors ad suggested.

Giskes glanced at the photographs, and immediately cognized van der Giessen and Rietschoten. He only asked ne question: "How are they to leave the Netherlands?"

"By submarine," Christiaan answered.

"Well, send them on their way, afterwards give us a port on how the English operate this escape."

He did not add that it might be used in the future to nd Abwehr agents to the United Kingdom.

Unfortunately for Krist, within 48 hours everything had hanged. Captain Wurr learned that Van der Giessen and ietschoten were taking a films with them, and it was thought at the films were of German installations at the mouth of e Maas, the Scheldt, or of the Zealand Islands.

This changed everything! The Germans had wondere
if the Allied plan to invade the continent consisted of sever
operations in regions considered to be particularly vulnerab
and important. Perhaps now they had the means of discove
ing the answer. Therefore, they could not allow the tw
men to escape —even at the expense of losing a possib
future route to Great Britian for German agents. They ha
to be stopped, the films taken—and the earlier the bette

Naturally Colonel Giskes did not feel obliged to infor
Christiaan about this change of plan.

Christiaan and his charges therefore took the train fo
Berg-op-Zoom, traveling in separate compartments for s
curity. Alone, Christiaan let his thoughts run freely. H
doubted that London would arrange a pick-up for Riet
choten and van der Giessen. This was surprising becau
the SOE must have realized that they were risking the
lives every day they spent in the Netherlands.

Later, Major Dobson—who replaced Major Bingham
the Dutch Section—tried to explain his criminal negligenc
He claimed that since the SOE had been brought up to da
on England Spiel, it had been extremely suspicious of escape
prisoners who could easily have been turncoats.

The more probable explanation was that when they realize
the extent of the England Spiel catastrophy born of the
negligence and stupidity, the ostriches among the SOE ha
an idea: they must ensure that the survivors would n
return to tell their story—at least until the end of the wa

If van der Giessen and Rietschoten had returned
England, they would not have been alone. Dourlein, Ulbric
Dessing would have at least confirmed their story, an
there might have been an investigation. Radio messages r
ceived from the radios of the Holland Plan since the begi
ning of the operation would have been studied—revealin
how Lauwers had risked his life to warn London that h
had been caught and forced to change sides. After that, the
would have parachuted a team of investigators "blind" (n
advance radio alert to the Resistance which could alert th
Germans too) which would soon have discovered the who
truth. But the SOE wanted to avoid a scandal at all cos
and an investigation would have caused a scandal!

As a direct result of this attitude, Van der Giessen an

Rietschoten were traveling to Zealand with Christiaan, under dangerous conditions. Sensing this danger, Christiaan became agitated and restless. A million questions came into his overheated mind. Would Giskes change his mind? Why had his superiors had the stupid idea of telling the Abwehr? Why hadn't England accepted the pick-up straight away? Did they want to prevent the escape? Did they hope the men would remain in the Netherlands? He did not dare go any further and wonder whether they hoped they would be recaptured but, unconsciously, this was his real worry.

Suddenly he stood up—to the polite surprise of his neighbours—and disappeared into the corridor, limping as he always did when troubled. He arrived at the compartment holding his two "parcels." The pair were surprised at the look of despair on Christiaan's face and wondered what could have made their guide ignore the security rules.

When the train stopped at the frontier of Zealand, uniformed Germans began checking the passes. Christiaan studied them. Two were wearing the uniform of the Gestapo!

The Gestapo! Giskes had betrayed him! He did not even have the courage to do the job himself. Oh no! The Abwehr did not do such work! The dirty jobs were left to the Gestapo, to the infamous Gestapo, and the Abwehr shut their eyes. Christiaan lowered his head.

They had betrayed him, everyone had lied to him, tricked him. They had assured him that everything would run smoothly . . . The Germans moved slowly toward him, going from compartment to compartment. They did not hurry. They were not in a hurry. Nobody could escape. . . . Nobody . . . was that certain?

Christiaan opened the compartment door, seemed about to shout something, but it was too late. The carriage was guarded at both ends. Leaving the door open, Christiaan silently went back to his seat. Behind him, in Reitschoten's and van der Giessen's compartment, a harsh voice asked for "papers." There was a brief silence and then:

"Ah! They are false! These are false papers. . . . The stamp —there, very badly imitated! Terrorists! Be quiet! Get up, put your hands up! *Schnell! Rauss!* Follow us!"

Christiaan gripped the leather arm rest. He heard cries,

the pounding of boots, the banging of doors. All this re-
sounded in his head, in his heart. He had never been so
ashamed. Those who had tricked him into this butchery
would never realize what they had done to him. It was
terrible, unbearable. Slowly, the train set off again, this time
without the two escaped prisoners.

But Krist, what was he still doing there? All that was
left was for him to return to Amsterdam or to Brussels.
Anywhere. He no longer had anything to do in Zealand.
It was finished, completely finished.

Suddenly Christiaan felt his reason waver. He no longer
understood! Those two—van der Giessen and Rietschoten—
they were resistants, friends. Why had he been told to take
them with him, if they were not to be allowed to finish
the journey? Why this atrocious comedy? What was London
planning? Or Berlin? Why was he made to do such work?
Why let them be arrested now? What was he doing on this
train in Berg-op-Zoom?

He wanted to go far away, never to return. What was
preventing him from taking the Spanish route alone? He
had had enough! He could go on no longer—somebody else
could take his place. He bequeathed it to them with all his
heart. The Spanish route! He had taken it so often, he knew
it so well! Yes, this was what had to be done. He would go
to London, he would explain to his superiors there. He had
friends. There was Kas de Graaf. He would tell him everything, and Kas de Graaf would straighten things out. Holland
was worth nothing to him. It had disgraced him. It was
finished, he was going to leave.

He never did.

Giskes was happy with his catch. The films found on
the two men were of all the German defenses in the Netherlands, including the launch sites in The Hague region: the
secret of all secrets!

The Gestapo was also jubilant. They took their revenge.
The prisoners were taken back to Haaren for "interrogation."
After that, they would be transferred to Assen and detained
as "enemy agents." The security rules at Assen were far
stricter than at Haaren.

But on June 9, 1944, the Germans changed their minds.
Instead of sending the two men to Assen, they took them

to the concentration camp at Vught. Because of the condition of the men after their "interrogation," they were taken by car. As soon as they arrived in Vught, they were executed. "Killed while trying to escape" was the official version.

A few weeks after the death of Rietschoten and van der Giessen, many of their captured compatriots in the Holland Plan were transferred to Mauthausen where they were executed in turn.

Christiaan was never officially informed of the extermination of the resistants, but he guessed as much. When he returned from the expedition, Giskes had summoned him to Dreibergen. King Kong obeyed the order, reluctantly.

He disembarked at Amersfoort as ordered. A car was waiting for him. He did not even have time to see the old chateau; he only just had time enough to notice that the little station smelled of spring, that there were flowers on the dunes and the wind sang in the pine forest. There in the middle of the forest was an isolated house which the car approached by complicated detours. It was here that Colonel Giskes had taken up residence.

Giskes, assisted as usual by Wurr and Willy, was prepared for reproaches but was not expecting him to be in such a black temper. He refused everything they offered him: a seat, a cigarette, a drink. He had come to report, he said, and had no wish to delay. Then, as they did not seem to understand him, he took out the 9 mm colt that Willy had given him some time before, at his request, and started to examine it carefully, unloading and loading it, aiming it, checking the safety catch.

Finally, he sat down in front of the table around which the three Germans were sitting. He sat stiffly in his chair and stared at Giskes with such hatred that the latter thought for a moment that his last hour had come.

The atmosphere was so tense that Giskes got up and went to his desk. He took a gun out of the drawer—a 12 mm American colt—and kept it in front of him during the whole interview, just by his hand, next to his cup of tea!

"I suppose you are satisfied?" Christiaan asked. Giskes tried to convince him that it was all at the Gestapo's initiative. According to him, the Abwehr respected King Kong's wishes, but there must have been a leak in Christiaan's network. Perhaps someone had told Schreieder that false papers had been obtained for Van der Giessen and Reitschoten? After that, of course, Kriminalrat Schreider would not rest until he had succeded in bringing back the prisoners, dead or alive.

At first, Christiaan refused to believe this story. But he was not strong enough to withstand Giskes. After all, the story was plausible—Giskes had had several days to prepare it. Willy and Wurr supported him as best they could. Among the three men, they had an answer for everything.

Finally, Christiaan had to admit that a leak from his network was not impossible. He remembered that his superiors in the Resistance had not seemed very worried about the future of Rietschoten or Van der Giessen.

Christiaan could not get this out of his mind, which put him on the defensive with Giskes. Without knowing the reason, Giskes noticed this and immediately pressed his advantage.

He changed the subject suddenly, as if he considered it closed: "You are on good terms with the CSVI groups, I believe?"

Christiaan answered automatically: "Yes, why?"

"One of them has just received arms and a secret transmitter. Do you know which one?"

"Yes," Christiaan admitted. He guessed that Giskes knew as much.

"Well, then, tomorrow, in a car which we will provide, you will gather all of the shipment and bring it to me. As I have often said, I don't want Holland to be transformed by the idiots in London into a closed field for civil war."

"The radio transmitter too, or only the arms?"

"Only the arms," Giskes gave a nasty smile. "The Gestapo want to keep the radio, to turn it. It will, of course, make a mess of things, but what do I care about that."

"There will be no arrests, this time?"

"No, not by the Abwehr, in any case."

But Christiaan would not be fooled again. He would carry out the mission—if his superiors were in agreement—but this time he would warn his friends of a possible raid.

Poor Christiaan was not clever enough! His superiors were

prepared to loose a bit of equipment to have him remain valuable in Giskes' eyes. His friends were not overworried by his warning. "Another whim of Lindemans who wants to get ahead," they said . . . up to the moment when the raid actually took place.

Luckily for him, Christiaan did not know about the raid and that several of his friends had allowed themselves to be caught in spite of his warnings. He was in Antwerp, where he was helping set up of the apparatus for the Resistance's plan to free the port. For a while he was happy, but this did not last. Giskes was about to have one of his brainstorms. The leader of Abwehr IIIF was beginning to lose his professional self-control.

He asked Christiaan to go to the editor of the *Christofoor,* a clandestine newspaper, posing as the leader of the Belgian Resistance Council. In this capacity, he was to offer the editor seventy carrier pigions to correspond with London. Thus Colonel Giskes hoped once again to sabotage the network communication with Great Britain.

But where England Speil had succeeded beyond expectations, the *Christofoor* affair was improvised and badly planned. For instance, if a Resistance Council (RVV) really did exist, no Belgian network had heard of it; and it was absurd to think that an underground leader would accept seventy carrier pigeons to correspond with the United Kingdom without first checking the source. The English did not use these birds at all except in very special cases. They sometimes gave *one* to an agent for him to free as soon as he arrievd to let England know that he had. But, *seventy!*

Christiaan accepted this mission for the Abwehr, convinced that it would fail. In fact, the editor of *Christofoor* hurridedly demanded explanations of London. His reqeust for information found its way to the BBO, and ended up on the desk of Kas de Graaf, who must have appreciated the essence of the situation and realized that, if his memories of occupied Holland did not betray him, the pigeons were flying toward certain death.

The *Christofoor's* message was worded as follows:

"A secret newspaper from Nord-Brabant tells me that a certain Krist, also known under the pseudonym of King

Kong, leader of a Belgian Resistance group, the Resistance Council, is offering us seventy carrier pigeons in order to communicate with London. Does King Kong deserve our trust? Do the pigeons really come from England?"

To which Kas de Graaf replied briefly:
"King Kong is boasting, as he always does."
The incident was, therefore, closed; the affair classified, the ludicrous episode came to an end without glory. Giskes and King Kong were thinking of other things.

King Kong's enemies waited. Helped by those resistants who were unaware of the role of double agent entrusted to Christiaan, they concocted a hurried warning for Kas de Graaf in London, bringing to his notice that Christiaan had been seen in the company of people like Jackie Breed, Aiby van Stratten and Albert Brinkman, three old CSVI agents who were said to have gone over to the enemy—which was not at all certain.

Convinced that security should come before everything else, Kas de Graaf decided to send out a general warning to the Netherlands groups. If they were wrong, if Christiaan deserved their trust, there would be plenty of time to give him justice later. But, meanwhile, they could not be too careful. He drew up the following telegram:

"To all networks. Cut contacts with King Kong. Change the addresses known to him. Understand."

And the answers were many. Some simply told of the measures taken; others protested that the suspicions were unfounded. Then there was this message:

"Precaution taken. Warning too late for the *Christofoor*. Team arrested."

Those who accused Christiaan of being the originator of this trap had not thought of the improbability of their charges.

The *Christofoor* was a very old, established secret newspaper. For a long time, the German services in the Nether-

lands must have known all the important members of its
team. Hundreds of times, a thousand times, a massive arrest
could have ended its career. Schreider was certainly dying to
close this magnificent trap, but no doubt he was restrained
by Giskes. Then Christiaan, on Giskes' orders, tried the
"pigeon penetration," certain it would fail because it was
too stupid.

After that, what happened? Giskes was furious, and might
well have decided to take his revenge by giving the green
light to Schreieder.

Those who wanted Christiaan's destruction added, for good
measure, that King Kong had "dubious associates." Which
is exactly the type of charge against which it is impossible to
defend oneself.

Christiaan was a very active agent, and his "cover" was
that of a smuggler. It is really imposible to see how he
could have avoided "dubious associates."

Be that as it may, shortly after this incident the Gestapo
intervened, and Christiaan's enemies were almost rid of
him for good.

The Germans had been alerted that on a certain day, at
a certain time, an "eminent member of the Resistance"
would strike a blow against the Rotterdam Exchange Control office. The information reached Schreieder, who immediately set up a counter-operation. His agents surrounded
the office, suddenly bursting in to find themselves in the
presence of a man obviously determined to sell his life
dearly. A German agent fired first, planting a bullet in his
lung. A few hours later Schreieder was notified of the
capture of the agent—identified as King Kong! Giskes was
immediately informed and the two men met to plan an
"escape." Christiaan was badly wounded and therefore taken
to Zuidwal hospital, giving the Germans enough time to
concoct a spectacular "liberation."

Contrary to what was said later, Christiaan was not
aware of Giskes' plans. He was also unaware of those of
his friends!

On its side, the RVV—for the sake of the person who
had led the attack on the exchange office—found it necessary that King Kong should escape. For this reason, it had

even asked the help of Bob Celosse and of the four men
dropped by parachute with him on March 1, 1944.

They organized an attempt to free Krist which failed.
They then organized a more powerful attempt. As luck
would have it, however, the day when 47 resistants attacked
the prison hospital in an attempt to free Christiaan, Giskes's
men also tried to recover him. Then followed a battle which
was deadly for the Resistance. Nearly all of Celosse's men
were killed. The survivors did not know what to do with
Christiaan.

They thought that the Gestapo would try to retrieve him,
that it was therefore necessary to find him a very safe
hiding place, but one where he could receive the attention
that his state of health required.

He was certainly far from well. The doctor who saw
him in his temporary hiding place informed the Resistants
that the lung was not healing and that recent events had
not helped Christiaan's condition. It was therefore necessary to find him a shelter which did not involve a long
journey and where someone would agree to stay with him
to nurse him.

A young girl offered her services, to everyone's relief. She
was Elly Zwaan, who had been a messenger for Christiaan
and who, of course, adored him! She was gay, robust, a bit
plump but, above all, she knew about Christiaan and his
secret activities. She knew what she was getting involved
in when she furnished a retreat for him.

She took Christiaan home, hoping that as soon as he
was better, she would be rewarded for her courage by long
and tender hours of gratitude. She was to be cruelly disappointed. Christiaan proved to be a most difficult patient
and, later convalescent. Impatient, his moods changing from
exaltation to depression, he longed to be on his feet again.
Despite Elly's protests that he was not fully recovered,
Christiaan soon renewed his usual contacts.

He would come home exhausted by his escapades, refusing to talk about them, roughly refusing all offers of assistance, so that Elly, deeply hurt, asked him if he no longer
had confidence in her. He would then soften, briefly, give
her one of his old smiles and a caress, but he did not let
himself relax for long.

He was more and more impatient, nervous, irritable. He seemed to possess inexhaustible financial resources which astonished the girl. He spent a lot of money with such feverish haste that Elly was really worried.

"You're drawing attention to yourself. Even if you have got money, don't chuck it around. People will become suspicious and start talking. I promise you, you're going to stir up a lot of trouble."

"Don't be so timid," Christiaan replied, "You sound as though you're frightened of your own shadow."

The girl shrugged and gave up trying to reason with him. But when he brought a tommy-gun back to the house, she was really scared.

"What are you going to do with that?" she demanded.

"I'm going to put it in my briefcase. In future, I shall be strongly armed wherever I go."

"But it won't fit into your briefcase," she argued.

And in fact, the barrel of the gun stuck out and Christiaan carelessly wrapped it up in an old issue of *Signal*. Obviously, he was more worried about not being armed than about being stopped for walking about with a whole arsenal—the tommy-gun being the most recent acquisition.

When he announced that he felt completely recovered and left, Elly Zwaan was very, very relieved! She would never have dreamed that the day would come when she would be happy to get rid of Krist.

His haste was understandable. He had learned that the Gestapo had descended on the Hotel Montholon in Paris one night, when Gilou Lelup and his little girl were there. They had both been arrested! Christiaan wanted to return alone, without any witnesses to hinder his activities, because he had to see Giskes as quickly as possible and ask for his help.

The colonel listened in surprise. He knew Christiaan had several mistresses and was never surprised to discover new ones. But he had always thought Veronica was Christiaan's "fiancée", the woman in his life he always came back to. He had been moved (as far as it was posible for him) by the anguish with which Krist had spoken of the arrests of Veronica and Henk.

And now the story was being repeated with another

young woman—a singer and a dancer from Lille instead of Rotterdam—and this young French woman was "the wife" of Christiaan and the mother of their child!

Giskes nevertheless composed himself. Realizing that his agent would be of no use to him unless he gave him back his wife and daughter, he took a lot of trouble to obtain their freedom. Christiaan was immediately notified. But more was needed to reassure the young man, who had had a very nasty shock. He insisted on going to Paris himself to confirm that Gilou and the child were really free and in good health.

But, Giskes pointed out, it would be an impossible journey. The Paris-Brussels line was under attack by the Allies several time every day and nearly all the trains were diverted via Lorraine or Luxemburg. Colonel Giskes, who had no wish to lose his only good contact with the Dutch Resistance, did everything possible to dissuade Christiaan from attempting such an expedition. But to no avail. Christiaan laughed and said that he would be perfectly all right. There was very little risk involved, he said; the danger had been grossly exaggerated.

He left and returned a few days later as if nothing had happened, in an excellent mood, with no explanation for his high spirits. Giskes tried to make him say what good news he had heard, but he had no luck.

"He never furnished important information on the movements of the Allied troops or their projects," confirmed the head of the Abwehr IIIF after the war. But a good information officer is not easily discouraged, and Giskes was very stubborn. Leaving Brussels for an unkonwn destination, (which, it was later learned, was the Schloss Hillenrath) Giskes gave his last instructions to Christiaan Lindemans.

He was to await the arrival of the Allies, introduce himself to them as a Dutch network leader and collect as much information as possible for the Abwehr. He was to pass through the lines to make his report, present himself to the nearest German headquarters and ask for "Doctor Gerhardt." This password would give him immediate access to the PC of the Abwehr.

But now that Christiaan Lindemans was alone with his Belgian friends, he was going to fight in broad daylight. The years of deception were finished; he would fight in the shadows no longer. He forgot all the worst memories of his life as a resistant. He thought only of the future.

A savage happiness broke inside him. He found a British paratrooper's camouflage uniform and fixed to the shoulder pads the three stars of a captain. He was going to fight for Antwerp and at last take revenge for the bombing of Rotterdam.

CHAPTER ELEVEN

Christiaan's first contacts with his Dutch compatriots, recently returned from London, were without much warmth.

He was in Antwerp, about to leave on a mission to the Netherlands, when he met Colonel Oreste Pinto. Pinto was about fifty with something bothersome in his face. A man who had known his hour of glory when he contributed to the unmasking of Mata Hari. In 1944, he was part of the counterespionage services of SHAEF and was considered a skilled, tenacious and very able investigator. He liked all women and liked displaying his strength and skill. Most important, he was a man who disliked being contradicted.

Behind the fighting Allied Armies, an enormous mass of men moving towards the Netherlands, the security of the communications lines and the freed areas had to be assured to sustain the fighting troops. It was not an easy task, and Colonel Pinto put everything he had into it.

In Antwerp, overrun by an oddly assorted crowd of homeless refugees, collaborators in flight, enemy agents, and members of the Resistance, it was decided to put all the displaced into one gigantic camp in order to sort them out and trace their backgrounds. It was similar to such places that

148

functioned in England during the war but much more rudimentary. The camp was surrounded by barbed wire, guarded by armed sentries. In a separate building, the security officers interrogated the internees, freeing those who appeared to be genuine patriots.

In front of a camp entrance, a giant in a captain's uniform, armed with two black steel knives, a luger, machine-gun and hand grenades, surrounded by about fifty young admirers, was discussing with the guards the possibility of the immediate release of two young girls for whom he was willing to vouch. Annoyed by this irregular intrusion in his domain and by the captain's stars which had obviously not been worn in the traditional army, Colonel Pinto approached the little group, took the officer aside and questioned him. He was not satisfied with the answers. His subject was noticeably unhappy about the questions. The two did not speak the same language. Christiaan Lindemans was exasperated by this small, dry man who spoke ironically about the usefulness of "irregulars".

That day a dangerous antipathy was born between these two. Pinto widened the breach by taking charge of a security check on King Kong. He claimed later to have conclusive evidence that Lindemans had been made to change sides by the enemy not at the time of his brother's arrest but much later when he was himself arrested. For good measure, he added that Krist "ran after girls without conscience or morality," and that his Resistance exploits had only been a cover for his renegade dealings, or simply stories.

A curious moral judgment from a man whose own private life was, to say the least, "irregular." He had been accused by his superiors of having had intimate relations with women "with whom he dropped his guard" even though they were, beyond doubt, enemy agents.

It was whispered that in addition to the animosity that sprang up between Christiaan and Pinto, a certain amount of rivalry over women did not help matters. Besides this, Pinto seemed to suffer from a persecution complex.

When he summoned Christiaan to his office in Anvers, he was told by the Prince's HQ that if his "suspect" was unable to come, it would be because he had left on a mission. Pinto was furious. As he had rather strained relations with the headquarters of Prince Bernhard, he immediately held him

responsible for this crime of "high treason," stating that
although he knew of the suspected treachery of Christiaan
Lindemans, Prince Bernhard preferred to shut his eyes to it
rather than admit that this war hero was really a hired enemy
agent. After this, Pinto swore that he would not rest until he
had proved the allegations that he had really only thrown at
random under the influence of his jealous temper.

Unfortunately for Christiaan, Pinto was not the only one
who felt vindictive towards him. At the Chateau Rubens, the
HQ of Prince Bernhard (who later transferred his HQ to the
Chateau Wittouck), where a conflict was developing among
the members of the different Dutch information services, it
was decided to sacrifice Christiaan Lindemans. It was merely a
question of waiting for the right time.

Only one man, it seems, took the trouble to try to search
out the true facts. Captain Kas de Graaf, though shaken by
what he heard, made a deserving effort to separate fact from
fiction.

Meanwhile, Christiaan Lindemans was wandering about
the Netherlands where he had a lot to do. On top of his
Resistance work, he had decided to pay his family and the
most charming of his mistresses a visit. At the same time, all
the information services were trying to get in touch with him.

Major John of the Dutch and Belgian sections of SHAEF
got the simplest idea of how to find Krist and thus set in
motion an avalanche of catastrophies!

He asked Elly Zwann to act as a courier. They furnished
her with a ferryman, and she set off courageously. However,
her guide was killed "by mistake" on the way and the young
girl, having no other means of entering occupied Holland,
sought assistance from Captain de Graaf, whom she knew as
a friend and old network mate of Christiaan.

Furious that SHAEF should have manipulated his own
services without telling him, Kas de Graaf made a bargain
with Elly.

"I'll fetch Christiaan myself," he told her. "I'd like to see
him again. But I think it's unlikely that he would be in the
Netherlands. He was seen recently in Belgium and also here
at the Prince's quarters. I think it's possible that he is still
here. As you who know nearly all his contacts, help me to do

the rounds. With both of us, it shouldn't take us long to contact him."

Elly Zwann, unsuspecting, agreed. It did not occur to her
that Kas de Graaf might have a darker motive for a meeting
with his old friend—until she found herself in the company
of Colonel Pinto who, probably intending to frighten her,
hinted she should "break all relations with Christiaan." This
was a clumsy blunder; he did not see that the young girl was
devoted to Krist.

Without the knowledge of the various Resistance organizations who were trying to lay their hands on him, Elly Zwaan
attempted to meet Christiaan. This she finally managed to do.
She put him on his guard against the animosity that Pinto
felt for him, the atmosphere of vague suspicion which reigned
in the Prince's quarters, adding that even Kas de Graaf
seemed to be influenced by all sorts of rumors that were
going around about Krist.

In an outburst of emotion, he cried: 'Traitor! What did
you tell them at the Prince's headquarters?'

'Was I wrong?' asked Elly anxiously. Then she explained
the conditions that had made her contact Kas de Graaf, whom
she had taken for a friend. She was nearly crying and her
distress moved Krist. Recovering himself, he smiled and said
softly: "It doesn't matter. Stop tormenting youself and look!"

He shoved under her eyes a crumpled piece of paper signed
by Kas de Graaf. It read: 'King Kong is all right.'

"You see?" he concluded. "You misunderstood."

"I promise you I didn't! Colonel Pinto. . . ."

Christiaan shrugged his shoulders, as if he feared nothing
and nobody, but it was obvious that he had suspected for some
time now that some sort of plot was being hatched against
him. If not, why would he have asked Kas de Graaf for this
half safe-conduct? This sort of document seems to have been
used quiet frequently during the Second World War, and had
become a practice of double agents when they were afraid of
being confused with enemy agents.

Nevertheless, Elly insisted: "If all is well, why is it so difficult to find you? Why don't we see you more often at the
Prince's receptions?"

"Because I was on a mission, my dear. You should know
by now that our work demands the maximum caution. I will

go to the Prince's quarters when it is convenient for me. Any
way, I attend receptions as little as possible. I hate playin
the circus bear for an audience which wants to meet resist
ants."

"They say they have a mission for you," murmured th
young girl, crestfallen.

"If it's true, they have a peculiar way of going about it
They make all the networks look for me with such discretio
that one would think they wanted to warn the Germans, i
case they miss me!"

This was highly probable in fact. The assault on Arnhem
had just taken place; the English were beaten and bitter. A
scapegoat was needed. Why not Christiaan? They didn't lik
him. He came from a family without social importance, h
already knew too much about the England Spiel and, as lucl
would have it, he was found in the combat zone at the ver
moment of the battle.

If he had fallen into an ambush during a mission, it woul
have been easier for everybody. But he was not dead. It wa
therefore necessary to mount—with every scrap of evidenc
available—an accusation against him.

Now, for whom was this honor being reserved? For one o
the information officers from the Prince's quarters? Someon
Christiaan did not know, who had never seen him? Not at all
They chose for this task Kas de Graaf, reasoning "that h
had known Christiaan better than most."

The inquest was rigged from the beginning, choosing a mar
who could not be completely detached. Any civilized tribuna
would have thrown the case out of court. It would have dis
missed Kas de Graaf from the inquiry, because he had beer
King Kong's friend and because Christiaan had saved hi
life. Such a man could not be objective. He would either reac
with horror and dismiss the charge because of sentimenta
reasons, or if he was a man of honor like de Graaf, he migh
lean too far the other way—not to be accused of favoritism
In any case, he would be easy prey for the intrigue that wa
steadily building up against Christiaan.

Three times, at least, Kas de Graaf summoned Krist to the
Prince's headquarters for official questioning, which wa
merely presented as a rough précis after the event and which
was held in a most irregular way. Officially, Christiaan Linde

mans was simply informed that he was only being asked to report on his past missions before new ones were assigned him. But one would have had to be made of stone not to sense the atmosphere of these sessions. The word, therefore, passed round rapidly that it was only a front, that they were trying to make Christiaan responsible for a certain number of disasters and "accidents," the most important of which was the betrayal of Arnhem.

The whole Resistance in the Netherlands, France and Belgium received the news with amazement and indignation. The Belgian National Movement, the White Brigade, the French FFI, the Secret Army, and many others made known what they thought in the clearest terms. Only the English remained quiet, and yet only they knew the truth.

Christiaan, a double agent?·But, of course. Everybody had known it for a long time. But they had also known that he had not liked doing it, that he had done it for his country and at the request of his own people. A "good double" was what Christiaan had been. What did they hope to achieve by deserting him? For whom were they trying to cover up?

Christiaan himself did not seem to have asked himself so many questions. Or perhaps he had thought his superiors would screen him *in extremis* and that the truth would come out. Even though he knew he was suspect, even though he was surrounded by indignant friends offering their help, he stubbornly waited for the interrogators to clear his name.

He could so easily have taken refuge in a neutral country, he had the means to do so. To cross the frontier was still easy for him. He could, like many doubles, have taken refuge under the wing of an Allied service which would have been pleased to take him on and give him a new identity after changing his appearance.

After all, why not? He liked the adventurous life. He did not particularly fancy returning to the narrow existence of his family, his garage and his old friends in Rotterdam. The post-war story is alive with such examples. People like Richard Christmaan, Gehlen, Cornelis Verloop and Otto John took this route. Why didn't Christiaan?

That is why, despite the advice of his friends and offers of help, on about September 23, 1944 (the Dutch are peculiarly vague on the exact dates of what happened during the period

immediately after Arnhem), for the first—but not the last—
time, Christiaan Lindemans reported to the Prince's headquarters and, hearing that Kas re Graaf wanted to see him, he
was filled with joy. Relieved, delighted and certain at last
that his innocence had been established.

The two men were to meet at the guard corps where Christiaan was made to wait until they notified Kas de Graaf of
his arrival. De Graaf drove to the meeting place, jumped out
of the car. Christiaan greeted his friend with great thumps on
the back: "Hello, old man! At last! I *am* glad to see you again.
I assure you I have asked myself more than once if we would
ever meet again."

Then silence fell between the two old friends. Krist, wide-
eyed with amazement, scrutinized Captain de Graaf, who
remained unmoved, whose face only expressed disapproval,
almost as though he had wanted to put Krist on his guard,
make him understand that he was lost, that nobody could do
anything for him. That if he wanted to stay alive, the best
thing he could do was to disappear—and quickly!

In fact, incredibly during this period, although he was
suspected of treason and despite the questioning at the Prince's
headquarters, they had not even put him under arrest. It was
as if they wanted to frighten him, make him flee, to make him
understand that he "was finished." Perhaps they lacked sufficient proof to support the accusations, or perhaps they knew
they were false and that they were relying on Christiaan's
flight to make things easier for them.

But as Krist did not seem to understand what they expected
of him, Kas de Graaf merely shrugged his shoulders with a
weary gesture and made a signal for him to follow him. One
in front of the other, the two headed in complete silence for
the chateau. They had nothing more to say to each other.

As they passed the telephone office, Kas de Graaf stopped
for a minute, put his head through the gap in the door and
asked them to send a few officers to his office: Captain de
Jong, Colonel van Hauten of the Sixth command, in particular. He had no intention of carrying out the questioning alone.

Then the two men walked up the first floor, seated themselves comfortably in armchairs and smoked their cigarettes.
Breaking the silence, Krist asked sadly: "What am I doing
here? Why have you summoned me? They told me I was to be

entrusted with a mission. Now I see it wasn't true. You simply wanted to ge me here, and now I have come, why do you seem so embarrassed?"

"You're dreaming," de Graaf replied. "We really have a mission for you, a very important mission. We are going to go over the details with a few of my officers whom I've notified and who'll be here shortly. But while we're waiting tell me what has happened since our separation? What happened to you?"

"What's the good? You won't believe me."

"You mustn't say that. It's your silence which makes you look guilty."

But Christiaan remained silent. He had nothing to say. They treated him like a suspect. They wanted to make him talk, to reveal his secrets, to make him fall into a trap so obvious that a six-year-old would have realized it!

In fact, the interrogations were very odd. No one took any notes and, according to Kas de Graaf himself, "all the important questions which were put to King Kong had been recorded, as well as the answers to his questions"—which leads us to believe that his interrogators established themselves as judges of what was "important" and of what was not. The embarrassment that the commission of enquiry officers must have felt, is shown by such expressions as: "King Kong's answers to the numerous leading questions he was asked can be considered satisfactory . . . but it was nevertheless difficult to believe that one could trust him", "The controllable answers . . . were consistent with the truth . . . one really felt this man was teling the truth," "Captain de Graaf, after his conversation with King Kong, had the impression this man was not a traitor."

Christiaan played their game. He at last understood that he had lost, that a double was defenseless against those who wished to make him out to be a traitor.

When a double is involved in exchanges of information with the enemy and is sent on operations for the enemy, how does one decide when and where the double has, or has not, gone too far? How does one decide whether he has given more than he received?

Still, Christiaan for a long time refused to believe they were going to sacrifice him, that they wanted to be rid of him.

Deep down he knew, but he did not really want to admit it to himself. As a test of the good faith of his judges, he suddenly asked: "Well, then, and my mission? Why aren't we talking about it?"

"We will see in a few days. There's no hurry."

"But where am I to wait?"

"Wherever you want. Where you usually stayed when you were in Brussels."

"But—I've no more Belgian money," he stammered.

Then he made a last cry, a last appeal, one last effort to conjure up the past. But in vain. At the end of the first of his "interrogations" a thousand Belgian francs were thrust at him by De Graaf and he left. Until his next interrogation he had nothing to do but to wait. He threw his money around as usual, and boasted of his exploits to the soldiers at the Prince's HQ. He swaggered in front of the resistants, the indifferent, everybody—because this was his way of covering up his resentment and his pain.

He was still free. Men like Dr. Somer and Mr. van Houten still refused to believe his guilt. When he was summoned to the Chateau Wittouck, he arrived very quietly, answered the new questions that had been concocted for his benefit. He answered patiently, tirelessly, as if he hoped to eventually tire his tormentors.

Meanwhile, he made no move. He appealed to nobody, he did not even ask for sanctuary and protection from men such as Captain Baker or General Neave. He was becoming bored. He had nothing to do in Brussels and time passed very slowly.

He decided to have a change of air. Perhaps he also wanted to show those who claimed to judge him that he could disappear how and when he liked.

Veronica was dancing at the Tabarin in Paris. Christiaan went to see her! This was typical of him. Whenever he was out of luck, he needed a woman. And in Veronica he had a woman and a friend, someone he had loved and who remained the trustee of his childhood memories.

What did he say to Veronica? Did he confide in her? Did he complain? Or was he silent, making the most of a last respite, only wishing to forget, to withdraw to the past? Did he ask the young woman for help? Did he ask her to vanish with him, to start a new life elsewhere. It is extremely improbable, for after a few days he returned to Belgium.

It was now the end of October, and for nearly a month the officers at the Prince's HQ had treated him as a suspect, searched his past hoping to find something which would embarras nobody else and which could seem to prove his guilt, but in vain. They did not dare arrest him. They had no concrete evidence.

Now it seemed as if they were counting on his quick temper, counting on him to do something desperate: to commit suicide perhaps, or at least to try to escape. But he continued to wait, with peculiar patience, hoping, no doubt, that things would work out. A strange situation, nothing but interrogations which resulted in unsatisfactory answers. Christiaan Lindemans, having finally realized that they were hoping to break him, did nothing—absolutely nothing—to defend himself, or find a new master, as any double could do if he really wanted to.

CHAPTER TWELVE

By the end of October Colonel Pinto had settled at the Papegaaienlaan, in Eindhoven. There, on instructions from SHAEF, he questioned agents who were crossing the front lines. Every day messengers arrived from the occupied zone with escaped prisoners, messages, requests, all sorts of news. To sort out, to collate his men's reports, to judge the value and authority of these reports was Pinto's job.

On October 27, 1944, they brought a young Dutchman called Cornelis Verloop to him. After three hours of questioning he finally admitted, according to Pinto, to having worked for the Abwehr.

What happend between these two men who both knew and hated Christiaan Lindemans? We only have the story that Pinto told the enquiry Commission.

"I know who you are," Verloop was alleged to have declared. "You're the Commanding Officer, Pinto, the head of the secret service (sic). Among your commanding officers are Captain Baker, Captain Le Jeune, Captain Lagas, Sergeant Moonfoot, Sergeant Rensing and Sergeant Dieterse."

This was, in fact, Pinto's complete outfit. Apparently he

was taken aback for a moment, then he asked: "How do you know all that?"

"Kiesewetter or maybe Bader told me—one of the leaders of the Abwehr in the Netherlands."

"Who could have informed Kiesewetter?"

"It was King Kong. Four days before he gave away the Canadian positions too."

This version of the facts leaves a lot of questions unanswered.

First of all, how could Verloop have known from whom Kiesewetter—or Bader—had acquired this information? He was only a minor agent and nobody in the Abwehr would have confided in him on this subject. What would have been the point? Surely they would want to protect their sources? And why would Kiesewetter have boasted of knowing "the Canadian positions" (for Market Garden) "four days beforehand," (and not two, as was the case) thanks to King Kong?

No, the whole story sounds possible only if Pinto had promised Verloop something in exchange. It was a ridiculous story, but it was better than nothing and, up to now, the evidence against Christiaan was non-existent!

In any law court, Verloop's testimony would not have held out for five minutes. Any good lawyer would have immediately pointed out that Christiaan did not go to Dreibergen until two days before Market Garden was launched and that Bittrich had known about the Allied plans since before September 8. That Christiaan's actions, finally, were typical of those of any double agent who was being manipulated by his leaders.

Finally, we now know that Verloop was arrested, escaped, was recaptured, and then vanished. Nobody ever heard of him again, except Pinto who says that he met him in occupied Germany after the war and that he was in the service of British Military Intelligence.

However on October 28, 1944, Christiaan Lindemans was undergoing another of his interrogations at Prince Bernhard's headquarters when a communication from Colonel Somer was handed to Captain de Jong. It was from Colonel Pinto. It stated the deposition of Cornelis Verloop, and that was enough to jail Christiaan. An officer discreetly left the room where the interrogation was taking place. He telephoned Major Sainsbury, security officer of the 3rd SF of the 21st Army, and asked him to come with a detachment of armed MPs. As it would take Major Sainsbury about an hour to reach Chateau Wittouck, they sent Christiaan to Captain de Graaf's room, explaining that the interrogations were over, that they were satisfied with his answers and that they were now going to tell him the broad outline of his new mission.

Happy and relieved, but not terribly surprised for he had always maintained his confidence in his superiors, Christiaan cried out: "Well, then, that's it and when do I go?"

"Straight away. But first, are you armed?" asked de Graaf quietly.

"Of course not! You know very well that when I come here I leave my weapons with the sergeant who is waiting for me in the car."

"For this mission, you will need to be armed. Check yours before leaving."

"I always do. I never leave it to anyone else." Christiaan was bewildered.

Footsteps in the corridor. Now, for the first time, Kas de Graaf revealed that he knew about the meeting between Giskes and Krist at the Botanical Gardens. Krist seemed overwhelmed.

Kas said, "It was a big mistake. The first of many."

"You can say that again," admitted Krist with bitterness. "I would never have believed that it would be so distressing, nor that later I would be charged with committing betrayals and offences of all the other agents as well."

Then hope returned. Kas de Graaf had talked about the meeting at the Botanical Gardens. If he knew that, he must know everything—that Krist was not a traitor but a good Dutchman. A double, indeed, but a good double. That left one chance, one small chance. And Lindemans, who had never talked about his actions and who had up to then scrupulously observed the order of silence wanted to justify himself.

'Kas . . ." he began.

Captain de Graaf interrupted him: "Don't be an idiot. I won't believe you."

Defeated and furious, Christiaan flopped into his chair and waited.

Preceded by Major Sainsbury and Mr. Knight, in charge of the Prince's security, the military police entered the room and seized King Kong. They were enormously strong men, armed up to the eyebrows. A display of force which was ridiculous against one man unarmed who would not defend himself.

The detachment's commanding officer wanted to handcuff Lindemans but the cuffs were too small. Major Sainsbury was annoyed, but it was not his men's fault. Nowhere could they find handcuffs to fit King Kong.

On the day of his arrest, Lindemans descended the stairs in silence, surrounded by his escort. They put him in a waiting car and Kas de Graaf watched them drive away with the young man who had been his friend and whom the State had labelled a traitor.

All was not finished. The evidence against Lindemans was still meager. Only vague presumptions could be found and the evidence was full of coincidences. It was hoped that the English would have more success. They hoped to find firm evidence that the accused man "had betrayed Arnhem," and they did not want anything to be overlooked.

Christiaan Lindemans was sent to London by plane, carefully bound in case by some miracle he burst the thin lining of the cockpit and threw himself into the air. Then, in a house not far from London, the intelligence agents questioned him again. This lasted two weeks during which time the Special Branch of Scotland Yard found a set of handcuffs to fit him!

According to Colonel Pinto, Christiaan gave detailed statements, filling up twenty-four foolscap pages, each page initialled by "the accused." But the British refused to part with the Lindemans file and only furnished the Dutch Security Office with extracts.

However, it seems that the English only learned one thing from Christiaan, and that they already knew: somebody, before September 8, had told General Willy Bittrich that a large offensive was being prepared in the Arnhem direction. But this somebody could not have been Christiaan. Obeying the orders of his superiors, he had given Kiesewetter the information about Operation Market Garden, prepared by the Allies for the Abwehr, only two days before the operation was launched.

The young resistant was finally returned to the Continent and deposited with the Dutch authorities in Brussels, where the HQ of the military delegate was to be found. However, the

British services in Belgium had a better idea: they questioned the poor man yet again before finally handing him over to his compatriots.

By then Christiaan had changed quite a bit. He was tired, apathetic and docile.

He was at first jailed in the prison at Breda, where Colonel Pinto boasted about having interrogated him several times, plunging him into attacks of rage—which is quite easy to believe and reveals Pinto's sadistic tendencies.

According to Mr. Einthoven, head of the National Security at this time, Christiaan was "a witness of particular importance" because he basically knew all the escape networks. He was, therefore, continually subjected to interrogation. According to a doctor's opinion, he presented certain physical upsets, which was one of the reasons presented for not allowing the trial to be held in public.

It was equally impossible to nurse Christiaan in a good psychiatric unit.

In June, 1945, without any official case having yet been opened against him, Christiaan Lindemans left Breda for Scheveningue. There he learned of his mother's death and was plunged into a deep depression. He had lost a lot of weight, he was going grey. He had a greyish complexion and seemed to be afflicted with the beginnings of motor paralysis.

Contrary to what was said later, Christiaan was never detained at the Hotel d'Orange which the Gestapo had made into a torture center. He was interned in barracks arranged after the liberation of political prisoners. At first they put him in a cell, but he reacted badly to the solitude and tried to commit suicide by cutting his wrists with a razor. They transferred him to the prison hospital, which had a rudimentary psychiatric section where the prisoners were hardly nursed at all, but where they were together, often boasting about exploits that the Dutch authorities termed imaginary.

There Christiaan recevied long and frequent visits from officials of the National Security. They created so much comment among his fellow prisoners that they finally had to put him in a small room attached to the hospital which had a large bolt on the door and solid bars across the windows. He could not, they claimed, escape from there. By now Christiaan was so thin that the doctors thought he had tuberculosis and he was becoming more and more paralyzed.

Nurse Onder der Linden, a charming, romantic 25-year-old young woman from a good family, fell in love with Christiaan at this time. At least, that was what the Dutch authorities thought. It's more probable that the young girl pitied him and that she had been upset that, in two years, they had not found time to submit him to his judges. She had concluded that the sick man was innocent. Anyway, it was she who proposed an escape plan to Krist.

She would file the bars of his cell. An escaped prisoner, known as "the singing Rat," would reconnoitre the area and would try to discover a way of getting some sort of ladder that he could push against the wall of the prison, near the cell, so that Christiaan could slip down to the ground.

None of this would have been difficult it Christiaan had been in his normal state of health, but after such a long imprisonment he was weakened, emaciated, and by now almost completely paralyzed. When he dropped to the ground, he landed so heavily that a sentry was attracted by the noise, and took him back to the hospital in a pretty bad state.

However discouraged, however disappointed Christiaan may have been after this failure, he nevertheless shortly after regained hope. It was 1946; he had been a prisoner since 1944.

The English press which had only published a few brief articles about the case in 1944, took up the affair again. This time they were not restricted by any censorship. They wanted to know what had become of this Dutch officer who had been accused of betraying Arnhem and imprisoned in "the Tower of London." Was it true that he was still in prison without ever having been put on trial, without having the right to choose a lawyer? Was it intended that he finish his days thus, without his case ever being heard? The British Government replied that Christiaan Lindemans had never been in the Tower of London, that he had been handed back to the Dutch authorities a long time ago, so it was up to them to explain.

The journalists found this a little abrupt. They continued their campaign, not only in the United Kingdom, but on the Continent. They all asked the same questions. A Dutch officer had been arrested eighteen months before accused of high treason. Had he been tried? If so, what was the sentence? If not, what had become of him? Why had he not been put on trial?

It was a year since Einthoven had been named head of the Dutch National Security. He had discovered the Lindemans file, in 1945, a legacy of his predecessor, Mr. Derksema, and immediately had begun a campaign to obtain the trial of the accused. Mr. Derksema, he said, who had directed a cloak and dagger affair in London, had perhaps found these proceedings normal, but he did not. Added to that was the fact that the war was over and "big Dutch interests were at stake." The only way of saving face was to judge the affair in the normal manner. He was not at all discouraged by the number of answers which accumulated on his desk.

In June, 1945, Mr. Einthoven put the file in the hands of a member of the War Council who eagerly asked "for a full enquiry into the security risk." Einthoven then went to see the president of the War Council himself—Mr. Doornhos—in August, 1945, and insisted yet again that Lindemans should at least be handed over to an instructing officer.

Immediately the president of the War Council had backed down, making vague excuses about the difficulty of procedure. Special courts had just been created which were in charge of judging crimes and collaboration offences. Was Lindemans under the jurisdiction of these courts or of the War Council?

The problem, we will note, is not unknown to criminologists. It is admitted nearly everywhere in the civilized countries that where a law of procedure is concerned—as was the case here—whichever court would be to the best advantage of the accused should be the court by which he is tried. Mr. Einthoven realized that only one possibility remained: that of forcing the Royal prosecutors to settle the point. However, he had not accounted on their fertile imagination. They succeeded in avoiding the issue because they said that they did not know which court of appeal would be competent to try him. Bois-le-Duc? The Hague? Arnhem? Or another?

Another excuse was that they had access to an "expert" medical report that Christiaian Lindemans was not fit to appear in court and was exhibiting psychic disorders. However, hey did not entertain the question of transferring him to a proper establishment for mental patients. What was their reason for this? Were they certain that no medical commission would agree to the confinement? Or was it that they did not wish to see the poor man get well.

Therefore, after much beating about the bush, the Dutch government had gained a respite. The press dropped the questions and turned to something of more interest to the leaders. Poor Christiaan Lindemans was forgotten again.

The hope which had for a while awakened in him disappeared, and this time he told himself that he would never be out on trial—or be cured. That he would never get out of prison, that they simply intended to leave him to keep body and soul together in a prison hospital, surrounded by mental patients, collaborators and a few common law prisoners. He realized that if he became incurably mad he would be confined and forgotten. If not, they would quite simply speed up his death.

He was tired of creating scandals when he was isolated in a cell, tired of hearing the other prisoners telling the same old stories that everybody knew by heart, tired, especially, of slowly dying in prison. He told himself that his escape try had been a stupidity. He was no longer fit enough to attempt the adventure. Where would he go? Without his mother, without support, without money, who would take him in?

It was no longer the era of the Resistance, when there was always a network to take care of you. What weapon did he still possess? There was only one and it was his secret—the secret that kept him in Scheveningue.

If Christiaan had not been weakened by two long years of atrocious imprisonment, if he had not been surrounded by lesser men or—who knows—by people in his enemy's pay, he would have thought (or they would have thought for him) of the only possible solution: a well-organized escape, not needing any physical strength, a safe retreat for a while, the revelation of the truth to the press (who would have payed well to publish Christiaan Lindemans memoirs). He did not think of it.

He had cried, Onder had cried, when they had taken him back to the hospital after his abortive escape, but he now thought that that had been idiotic, that there did not exist, outside, a corner of the globe where he could rest his head.

One day he called Onder and drew her into a little niche in the hospital, murmuring: "Onder, you know that I am not a traitor, you believe me, don't you?"

"Yes, Krist," she said, "with all my heart."

"Well, that's not enough. God knows the truth. My little Mother who is now with God knows it also. And you, you know it, but nobody else believes me, you see."

"So, what do you want to do?"

"Do you love me, Onder? Do you really love me?"

"Yes, Krist."

"Then come close to me."

She came—with a heavy heart. It was an awful scene. Christiaan could not see himself as he really was. He thought he was still capable of seducing a woman. Onder pitied him, did not have the courage to take away this last illusion. That day she felt that the end of the road was not far off, that she would soon no longer need to pretend. His kisses had a taste of death.

She was right. After a moment he whispered: "If you love me as much as you say you do, give me some poison."

Onder de Linden hesitated. But at the bottom of her heart she had been waiting for such a request. Abandoned by everybody, betrayed, Christiaan Lindemans would never be put on trial. They had condemned him to this slow death in order to avoid a public hearing. After all, he had been arrested on October 28, 1944, it was now the end of July, 1946. In two years nobody had even found the time to hand Christiaan Lindemans over to a court judge, even for a first appearance, even to ask him to state his identity and to choose a defense counsel! It was one of the most shameful denials of justice in recent times!

And he was asking for poison. It was easy to find. Doctor van Stockun, a prisoner who acted as the hospital doctor, sometimes prescribed bromide for those who were agitated, or arsenic for the cardiac cases. Luminal was also part of his arsenal. He always had some on the trolley which the nurse wheeled every night from bed to bed before turning out the lights.

No, this was not the difficulty, but Onder clearly under-
od what the consequences of her action would be. She
uld never find another job. Perhaps she would be impris-
ed somewhere, like Christiaan. And what would her
nily say? Such a respectable, such a "well to do" family.
e could not refuse to show Christiaan this last charity—
d she could not outlive him. All she could do was die with
n.

Onder, therefore, wrote a last letter to her parents. The
uple said pathetic goodbyes. Christiaan had not foreseen
s double suicide. He did not want the young girl to follow
 example. But she was stubborn. Like him, she thought
t there was no longer any chance of justice. This revolted
r. She could only help him in this way: to die.

Somebody noticed the two thrown against each other, dying,
d warned the doctor. For Onder der Linden, no difficulty:
 ambulance took her to a hospital where they immediately
mped out her stomach. But Christiaan remained a prisoner,
criminal.

A ludicrous scene unfolded at his bedside: nobody knew
ere to send him to be treated, what establishment could
eive him. Meanwhile, the poison continued to do its work
d they wondered whether they could simply wait for the
n to breathe his last.

But this could not last forever. A hospital was finally de-
ed on, an ambulance came to fetch the dying man, robust
rses received the order to put him on a stretcher without
ay.

It was then that an incredible scene took place.

Christiaan, whom they thought already in a coma, sat up
 bed. His paralysis had vanished completely. He seemed to
ssess the strength of Samson. He shouted: "You've come to
ish me off. I know, I have understood."

At this, the other prisoners sprang up from their beds and
ristiaan, miraculously revived, did likewise. They dismantled
ir beds, pulling out the planks which they clutched as
apons.

The nurses moved back. They shouted to the prisoners to
 quiet, to Christiaan to let go of his plank, but they stood
 a safe distance, for the young giant was brandishing the
provised club like a bit of straw. They thought he would tire

himself out. They appraoched him stealthily intending to ta
him by surpirse. But he was on his guard, moving about lik
whirling dervish.

Several time he brought down his weapon on the heads
those who were attempting to seize him: doctors, warde
nurses. Bones cracked. Soon the floor was scattered with m
Some fifteen warders, attracted by the noise, surrounded
prisoner. He continued, none the less, to fight, in the joy
his recuperated strength, master of his destiny for the f
time in two years.

Two warders had also succeeded in getting hold of pla
from the battered beds. They started a grotesque duel w
Christiaan. One of them succeeded in hitting him seve
times on the head. His nose was bleeding, his teeth w
broken, but still he fought.

The unequal and shameful confrontation finished as s
denly as it had started. The other prisoners, exhausted,
themselves be subdued. Christiaan stood alone, swaying,
strength had left him. He crumbled on to the wreckage of
bed and lay still.

He was suffering from multiple fractures, concussion
fractured skull . . . and he had also absorbed eightly Lumi
tablets!

He died without gaining consciousness, without sayin
word. In their offices, the officials sighed with relief.

They whisked Onder der Linden away. After a rest, wh
she badly needed, they apparently provided her with a si
cure. Some even confirm having met her in Germany wh
she held "an envied position in the service of the Dutch g
ernment."

In 1950, Oreste Pinto, still full of malice, arranged to p
lish his version of the Lindemans affair in the *Sunday Dispa*
but The Hague forbade him to publish it. Kas de Graaf, us
the title of *Carnaval des desperados* (and under the pseudor
of Noel Degaulle) gave a highly coloured and romantici
image of the King Kong affair and of England Spiel. Fina
the enquiry Commission believed they were able to close
book on the controversies created by this lamentable adv
ture, bemoaning "the premature end" of Lindemans!

They now hoped that everything would be forgotten.

Those who attempt to open up the case again are not exa

helped in their research. But one day the Official documents concerning the battle of Arnhem will see the light. On that day we will know who warned Willy Bittrich, and Christiaan Lindemans will be cleared.

Action And Adventure From The World Famous EDGAR RICE BURROUGHS

The Efficiency Expert   18900-8 $1.95
Jimmy Torrance has finally found himself a decent job, but members of Chicago's underworld would rather see him behind bars.

The Girl From Farris's   28903-7 $1.95
Once a "lady of the night," Maggie Lynch desperately wants to escape her past. When she does go "respectable" she discovers that there is always someone who remembers.

The Deputy Sheriff of Commanche County 14248-6 $1.95
Although all the evidence points to Buck Mason as the killer of Ole Gunderstrom, he knows he is innocent. Now all he has to do is prove it.

The Bandit of Hell's Bend   04746-7 $1.95
Another unforgettable Western adventure by one of the master storytellers of all time.

The Girl From Hollywood   28912-6 $1.95
The hard but satisfying life the Penningtons lead on their ranch is shattered when a Hollywood drug pusher appears on the scene.

The Oakdale Affair   60565-6 $1.95
Two bizarre and seemingly unconnected crimes in a small town are woven into a fantastic story which will keep you guessing right up to the surprising climax.

Available wherever paperbacks are sold or use this coupon.

CHARTER BOOKS, Book Mailing Service,
P.O. Box 650, Rockville Centre, N.Y. 11571

Please send me titles checked above.

I enclose $. . . . . Add 50¢ handling fee per copy.

Name . . . .

Address . . . .

City. . . . . State. . . . . Zip . . . .

Ha

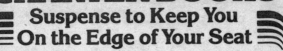